When Building a Billion Dollar Company

Here are a few things to think about

Richard Scrushy

When Building a Billion Dollar Company

Here are a few things to think about

ISBN: 1496171780
ISBN-13: 9781496171788

Printed in USA by (Create Space DBA of On' Demand Publishing, LLC)
Distributed by (Create Space DBA of On' Demand Publishing, LLC)
Editor (Create Space of On' Demand Publishing, LLC)
Acknowledgements (Friends that encouraged me to write this book)

Contact Information
www.RichardScrushy.com
www.7VENTHPOWER.com

Thank you to the shareholders of 7venth Power, Inc. who hired me as their president and CEO and paid me to write this book.

Richard Scrushy

Dedication

First, I dedicate this book to my lovely wife who stood with me for so many years through both trials and triumphs. It was her love that kept me going during the worst of times and her smile that motivated me in the best of times. She is a very special lady who has made me want to be the best I can be. I love you so much, Leslie.

I also dedicate this book to my parents who have passed over to the spiritual side. They made me strong, and they poured into me a desire to keep pushing no matter what kind of situations life dealt me. My parents believed I could do anything I desired to do. It was that drive that pushed me to build great businesses.

I must also dedicate this book to my wonderful children whom I love so dearly. They never stopped believing in their daddy, and you know that will keep a man working hard and striving to be successful. I would also like to thank my brother and sister for the love and support they gave me as well. They have always been there for me and my family no matter what we needed.

I have to mention the wonderful faithful people who supported me during the twenty years I was actively building companies. So many special people played a major role in the success of the companies I had the opportunity to build and be a part of. Many of them supported me through my trials as well. Those are the real friends, the ones you will always appreciate and love.

Lastly, and most importantly, I must mention my Father in heaven and my Savior Jesus Christ who gave His life for me. It is my belief and faith in Him that gives me the strength to do all I do. Without Him I am nothing and could do nothing. All good gifts come from Him. My ability to dream and to build companies comes from Him, and for that I give Him all the honor and glory for He is real and alone He is God.

Table of Contents

Dedication vii

Preface xi

Introduction xiii

The Idea, Vision, or Dream 1

Do the Math and See If It Works 16

Where Do You Get the MONEY? 28

Building YOUR Management Team 38

Mergers and Acquisitions 52

Things That Can Go Wrong 67

Taking It to the Top 72

Meetings and Encounters with Leaders and Winners ... 83

Making the Difference 102

When Blessed, Bless Others Make Sure There Is
    Balance in Your Life 111

About the Author 117

Preface

When we decided that I should write this book we had the discussion of what type of approach should be used to present this information to the reader. After much thought and discussion we decided to write the book as an informal conversation or a one on one coaching format. While building several large successful companies, I experienced the hardships and the victories and the processes that took us down both of those roads. We felt that a few of those experiences were worth sharing.

This is in no way a book that tells you step by step how to build your business and that is why we titled the book "WHEN BUILDING" and not "HOW TO BUILD" the BILLION DOLLAR COMPANY. We also added a second line to the title which simply says "HERE ARE A FEW THINGS TO THINK ABOUT" and that is what we wanted to share with you. A few things that may help you or inspire you as you go down the path of deciding to build your dream or to help you as you are in the process of building your vision into a business. Again our approach was to write the book for a broad audience and not for the business professor or the already successful business executive. The book is written for easy reading and not as a business school text book.

The business entrepreneurs in this country will build businesses of all different sizes both in revenues and geographic reach. They will come from all walks of life. Many will start out small and yet they will build their ideas into large billion dollar companies that will employ thousands of workers. Many of the great companies of our future have not been born yet and their visionaries may not have been born yet, but they are coming and we hope that this book will touch someone that will be the builder of one of the great companies of the future.

Introduction

This book was written for a wide range of individuals: those with the entrepreneurial spirit and a dream, those looking for an idea and who want to become a business builder and owner, those who already own a business and are trying to decide their future, business students who aspire to own and build a company, as well as people who just want to understand what it takes and what may be important when building a great business.

Much of the book was written from my studies and observations of CEOs of various companies as well as some of my personal experiences as I went through the trials and triumphs of building several businesses that grew to more than one billion dollars in sales and revenues. I not only wanted to document some of the processes but to help others who want to build their dream or fulfill their vision or idea of building a billion-dollar company. I realize that not all of the things that I have written will apply to everyone, but I do believe the book will make readers aware of many of the things that need to happen to build a business. This is not a story about any particular company that I have built or a story about me building any specific company but rather general information that applies to almost any business.

I also know that this book is not everything one has to know or everything one will be able to do. That was not the objective we had in writing this book. My hope is to provide inspiration to others so that they too can build a great business and a billion-dollar company. I hope that by sharing the processes as well as my experiences and those of other CEOs, you will realize that you can do this too. I believe this book will make it a little easier by giving you knowledge of what you may encounter along the way. Many times it is the unknown that keeps people from going forward with their ideas. The sharing of some of these experiences can open the eyes of others and show them that they too can do this. There is no cookie-cutter approach to building the billion-dollar company, but there are certain processes and phases that all companies go through. I attempted to put as many of these elements in this book as possible, along with some stories that will add a little color to the experiences.

You will have lots of your own stories when you build a large business. There will be times when you are down in the valley and times when you are on top of the mountain. I wanted the book to send the message that when difficult times come and you find yourself in the valley do not stop moving, just keep pushing and fighting and climbing until you are out of the valley and back on the mountain. I am a natural optimist, which is an asset in business. It is necessary; otherwise, you will find a lot of reasons not to do the tough and difficult things. Understand that if you get up earlier than others and work harder and smarter you can beat your competition and overcome large obstacles. That may be one of the most important things you should get from this book. What I didn't write about were the day-to-day things your staff will do in operating your business which are all absolutely essential in building a company.

We all know that these things have to happen and that qualified people have to do the work. I wanted to write about the things that I believe make the difference between building a small mediocre company versus building an industry leader that becomes a multibillion-dollar company.

one

The Idea, Vision, or Dream

Can you build your idea, dream, or vision into a billion-dollar company? The question is *how* do you build a billion-dollar company? Have you ever met someone who had a vision and built it into a billion-dollar business? Have you wondered if you could do that? What does it take to build a large successful company? God gives people visions, and we know this because in the scriptures in Joel 2:28 we find young men who were given visions.

In most cases God gives only one person the vision, just as he gave Noah the vision to build the Ark. However, confirmation will come as others give you an encouraging word to follow your dream or vision. Some may even prophesy what you need to do or what you are going to do. In my case God not only gave me a vision but He also gave me a burning desire and passion to fulfill my dream. Many say this is what makes someone an *entrepreneur,* a word derived from the French meaning one who is willing to take the risk of starting and building a business. I guess I fit the bill of an entrepreneur. Do you? Do you have a dream, a vision, or an idea that could become a booming business success story?

The word *vision* is used seventy-seven times in the Bible. The number seven means spiritual perfection. I believe this must have something to do with getting it right or doing the thing that is purposed for your life. I also believe for one to be a true entrepreneur he or she must not only have the vision or idea of the business but also mentally needs to see it operating and being successful. Of course this would be in his or her dreams. What I am saying is if you cannot imagine in your mind what the business will look like once it is operating, how would you ever know what to build? The same applies to a carpenter. How will he build a house if in his mind he cannot see what the finished product is supposed to look like? You may have heard the old saying "Any donkey can kick a barn down, but it takes a real carpenter to build one."

Starting a company from scratch is much different than buying an existing company that is already operational or taking over the management of a company that someone else has built. When you start with an idea and a business card and nothing else then you must have the vision and passion and be willing to do whatever it takes to put wheels on your dream and to make sure it has whatever it needs to grow and prosper. In teaching classes on starting businesses, I always ask the students what kinds of businesses they would like to start. So many times I find bad ideas where the skill set does not match the concept and where it is impossible to raise the capital required. Sometimes it's just not a good business. There are many different types of businesses, i.e., services, products, manufacturing, technology, etc. For example, carpet cleaning is a service business, and manufacturing and selling women's pajamas is a manufacturing and products business. Different businesses require different levels of capital. Capital-intensive businesses will require large amounts of equity along with some form of debt financing. Certain businesses have the potential to grow larger than others.

Can your concept grow to be nationwide or even worldwide? Will it be a chain operation? Will it expand nationally or maybe even internationally? If the answer to these questions is yes then the next question has to be can we finance it or raise the money to get it started? I must also ask this question: Is the concept proven? Will your company be a "me too" company? In other words, is someone already doing it? Later on we will talk about venture capital, and when we do you'll see the venture capitalist likes to be the first out of the box with a business concept or a product. They will fund a "me too" company if the industry has room, but you need to have a competitive product and a unique set of features and benefits that gives you a competitive edge and allows you to build a large, successful, and profitable business.

Does your business idea solve an existing need? How big is the need? Is it a local, regional, national, or international need? Is it a better way to do something? Is it a less expensive way to do something? If it is a product, does it eliminate an existing product by offering better quality? I could go on and on, but your business idea or product or solution needs to be really good, solve a problem, reduce cost, or improve our existence as humans. I know this is obvious, but there are certain businesses whose products and services we cannot do without. For example, we must eat; we need homes to live in, furniture to sit on, clothes to wear, transportation to go places, and health care when we are sick.

People will always buy these things. We know the car industry offers customers numerous options and so does the furniture business, restaurants, and grocery stores. Health care will always be a necessity in our lives, and there are many options here as well. However, there will be more new restaurants, more new car options, more new furniture options, and health-care technology will continue to advance and we will see more new diagnostic tests as well as new treatment options for various diseases and injuries. New ideas and better ideas in old industries and even repackaging those businesses can work well if it is a concept that is needed.

It may just be a better or more cost-effective way to do something. For example, when the MRI machine came on the health-care scene it gave the doctor more comprehensive information to diagnose the patient's situation. Therefore, the patient received improved health care. The MRI and CAT scan machines almost eliminated the need for exploratory surgery. This was a great leap in the practice of medicine, and these devices are much better today than when they first arrived on the market. They are also less expensive and they are the standard of medical practice. If a patient does not get an MRI or CAT scan when the patient needs it, a doctor could find him- or herself in a malpractice suit as a result of a misdiagnosis where the patient failed to receive the necessary treatment for his or her condition.

These machines are here to stay until the next new invention comes along that gives us more data faster and at less cost. Now let's take a look at the fast-food business. Is there room for another new concept? We have numerous options: hamburgers, chicken, pizza, sub sandwiches, salads, barbeque, fish and chips, and Mexican and Chinese food. There are others, but for the most part they fall into these categories. I believe we will continue to see new concepts because we like choices. Those new concepts will be competitive as well, but that is okay. The question is can you carve out a segment of the market share? Let's say it is possible. If you build a prototype and your overhead and expenses are $800,000 a year, for example, and you can bring in $1.2 million gross sales, then you would have a pretax profit of $400,000. This seems simple enough? Can you repeat this?

Why is your concept working so well? Is it just you personally? Can it work without you being there? Will it work in a town or area where no one knows you? Can we build a hundred or maybe even a thousand of them and get the same level of financial results or better? How many markets are there for this type of store or business? We are getting to the place where we begin to separate real big business opportunities from local one-store mom-and-pop operations.

We know there are many national and international fast-food companies that are multibillion-dollar companies. Look at all the hotel and motel chains. They range from the less expensive but clean models with free breakfast to more expensive models with spas and upscale dining. Many of these are multibillion-dollar companies. As we begin the dreaming process of how big we can build this business we must be very truthful with ourselves. What size market in terms of population will this business concept or store be able to operate successfully and achieve your revenue and profit goals? We also need to take a look at how many markets that size or larger exist. In the United States there are approximately three thousand counties and three hundred metropolitan statistical areas, or cities with a population of more than one hundred thousand.

You may also look for other specific requirements for each market, income levels, age, and mix of population, etc. It really depends on the specific type of customer you are looking for. For example, the hotel business looks for a certain type of market and fast-food companies do an excellent job of making sure the proper demographics exist in their target area. Conducting a traffic study to make sure the customers are there is a good idea. Population information is easily available today to provide you with all sorts of data, such as age, income, households, etc. There are maps that show areas of growth as well as areas where population is declining that you can obtain through local commercial real estate companies. The bottom line is before you run out with your idea, business concept, or dream and begin raising capital, do your homework and find out how big this business can be.

I had the wonderful opportunity to have dinner with Mr. Joe Bruno, the founder of a very successful grocery store chain called Bruno's. He told me that he had developed the ability to drive through a community or city and determine where his stores would be successful. He looked at the type of cars and homes in the neighborhood and counted the cars going down the street as well. He also studied the other businesses in the area.

If your idea is a product to be distributed through retail outlets owned by others then another approach is needed, but similar population studies are necessary. The studies need to reveal the number of customers in a particular area as well as how many retail distributors for this product exist in America. You also need to find out why the retailers would sell your product. If you have a product that will be sold to industry or directly to installers or wholesalers you will still need to determine how big this business could really be.

How many customers are in your universe? Run some back-of-the-envelope "what ifs" to determine how much the company would generate in sales if you reached 10% of the market.

Run several models using 5 percent, 10 percent, 15 percent, and 20 percent. If your analysis indicates that your business can be a nationwide company and generate hundreds of millions and maybe billions you definitely need to read this entire book. It will give you a lot of insight into my personal experiences building companies, several of which became multibillion-dollar companies. If your analysis indicates your business idea will not be able to generate these numbers, then go back to the drawing board either to rework your original idea or to come up with an entirely new idea.

The following chapters will take you through the processes of being successful and the potential mistakes you may encounter while building the multibillion-dollar company.

If you have a good concept and the drive and the passion to pursue this dream you can do it. I am living proof along with many others who have done it as well. I believe this book will save you time and money and give you some information that will help you accomplish your goals.

Every time I began to become passionate about building one of my dreams or visions I would share my idea with friends, family, business associates, and others. I would bounce the concept off of them, hoping to hear them say that it was a great idea. When I heard, "Hey, you should start a company doing that" from people who had a respectable business background, I thought I might be on the right track and would then proceed with the next steps: building financial models and projections and doing demographic studies, competitive analysis, and pricing studies.

Early on you will want to meet with an accountant and an attorney and maybe a couple of bankers to get their thoughts and reaction and begin to build relationships for the future. Before you talk with them make sure you have a full understanding of your revenue model and expenses, including who your customers are and how big the market is for your idea, product, service, or business. Also be able to discuss your competition and why your business is a better solution. If it's a new idea then be prepared to answer why anyone would need it, use it, or buy it. You should have some rough numbers in your head about these things as well as approximately how much capital you will need to get started, to break even, and to achieve profitability. You will need this basic knowledge when you talk to bankers, accountants, and other business people. If they do not ask you these questions, then go to someone who will. They may not understand enough about building a business to help you. There are accountants and attorneys who will encourage people to go forward just to get fees from them. Many times the businesses should never have been funded because the concept was faulty, and the investors, including the founder, lose their money when the business fails to get any traction.

Let's discuss "me too" companies and mistakes some people make. I was teaching an entrepreneurship class once and a lady in the class told me she wanted to open a children's shoe store, saying this had always been her dream. She didn't have a new or unique concept. I asked her where she was going to locate the store and she told me about a certain shopping center that happened to have a large department store as the anchor tenant, as most do. I was familiar with that location, and I told her that site already had a national discount shoe store, a national chain children's shoe store, plus the large department store that sold children's shoes. I then asked her how she would compete with those stores, and she said she hadn't really thought about that. She even said she wanted to sell many of the same brands the others were selling. I know this is a simple example, but the concept is the same no matter what your business is. Her little shoe store would have sold some shoes and she may have made a little money, but her return would never have been worth the effort. It would have been very hard for her to compete in those demographics. She probably would have burned up her cash and had to close the business over time.

However, if she had an exclusive on a new line of shoes that kids all over America couldn't live without—a new concept or fad, something hot that every child wanted—that is a different story. If this is the case we may need to raise some capital once our market studies prove that the product will sell. How many kids will buy them? What are the demographics? How much will they cost? What is the profit margin? Who will manufacture them? How durable are they? Will we own our own stores or will they sell in other retail stores? How do we get distribution? The questions go on and on. How will we brand these shoes? What is the marketing plan? What will the logo look like? Will we sell other types of shoes? Will we sell only to children? What will the critics and the foot doctors say? You can think of many more questions yourself. I think you can see we must thoroughly think through our idea or business in every way possible. You must ask the tough questions and get the answers before you take it out to the world. If the answers are not so good then do not force it. It may not be something you want to spend all your money and time doing only to lose everything.

This process is certainly part of building a large business. You may find your idea is only good in certain markets or only locally or regionally. Therefore, its revenue would be limited and it would never grow to be a large company. That may be fine if you want to run a regional or a local operation. There is nothing in the world wrong with that. But it does take a different approach to financing the business. In most cases it eliminates the interest of experienced venture capital funds and the investment bankers on Wall Street. The venture capitalist firm is looking for returns that get at least five or six times its investment in five to six years at minimum, but what the venture capitalist firm really wants is ten to twenty times its investment or more. The original venture capital investors in my first big company made at least ten to twenty times their investment—some may have made even more—and they did it in three to five years. Investment bankers are looking for companies that need their services to raise tens of millions of dollars to finance their growth. Local and small regional companies do not typically give returns that interest venture capital companies. However, there are some regional companies that grow to a size in terms of revenue, profits, and multiple locations that are able to go public as a NASDAQ or over-the-counter company.

Many businesses start out as single-store operations and then over time out of their own cash flow and with a little help from local banking begin to add stores. Before long they may find themselves with ten to fifteen store locations, each grossing one to two million with nice 20 percent to 30 percent operating margins. If these companies still have healthy growth opportunities in their regional market and they can show Wall Street that this growth is achievable and Wall Street agrees, then they get to play like the big boys. They get to sell their equity into the public markets, which is a much better deal for them than the private capital markets. It gives them access to less expensive capital to grow and allows them to reduce bank debt and borrow at much better rates, increasing the amount banks will lend them. Having the fresh infusion of cash from a public offering makes the local banks that loaned money to the company look like they were smart.

As a public company the original founders and investors will have an opportunity for some liquidity as well. After six months or so the new Wall Street investors will allow the founders to sell some of their stock and usually allow them to put millions in the bank. It is this reward that keeps the entrepreneurs coming and makes all the hard work worth it. Once they have some money in the bank and they know their families are taken care of they can now focus totally on building the business.

My point here is that it may be difficult for the small regional company to start with the experienced venture capital investor, but if they are successful they can still build a nice-size regional public company. Some of these companies will grow past their regional markets, but most will not reach a billion dollars in revenues. So as we think about our concept, is it regional? Is it national or international? I am not saying a regional company cannot achieve a billion in sales because it can. I am saying that most do not.

I was involved in the early life of a drug company that made painkillers. I went on the board when the company was a very small local concern and still not profitable. The painkilling ingredient in the drug was out of patent, but it was a much-needed drug for pain. The venture capitalist didn't initially have an interest because the drug was out of patent. After agreeing to put our own money in the deal, meeting with our management and hard selling them that they would get their minimum return, the venture capitalist finally agreed to invest a few million dollars. I guess you could say they returned a favor as well because we had involved them in other very lucrative deals. The company was able to raise the money and put the venture guys on the board and then they went to work. The CEO was a great guy with good experience in the drug business. He believed in this drug and this company. His commercial banker had sent him to me to help and advise him on raising venture capital. I liked him and the company and wanted to help him. I then got in touch with venture capital firms I had relationships with and had invested in deals with me in the past.

Once the deal was done the CEO took the funds and hired eighty or so salesman and began a nationwide strategy to build this company and sell some serious drugs. The revenues began to grow, and everything we promised the venture capitalists happened. The CEO saw his dreams materialize. The money was the key to kick-start this business. The CEO had a national company after only a few years, and then a major drug company made an offer we could not refuse. So the board decided to sell, and everyone made money. The venture capitalists got their return, and the CEO and the original investors, including me, made money.

That company was Russ Pharmaceuticals, and the drug was Loritab. No doubt they have made millions and millions off that drug as it is still a widely used painkiller. The hydrocodone found in cough syrup is the drug that was used in the Loritab that was then out of patent. It was the CEO who had the vision and the idea of putting the hydrocodone in the pill. It worked, it was brilliant, and it is still working today. Now this didn't fit the normal process of funding. I believe you could say it was outside the box of most deals. I bring it up here to show you that the passion and vision of the entrepreneur is important, and each successful deal has some unique process in it. This company sold products nationally, and I'm sure that if we had not sold the business the company would be a major pharmaceutical company today. Of course we would have had to grow our product line by adding more drugs. No doubt that would have happened. We were already beginning to look at other drugs that were available or becoming available. Now, it is highly possible to come across a mom-and-pop single-store operation that you fall in love with, an operation you believe could grow to a national business. It could be a single product or a single store, just like the drug Loritab that became a national product.

A few years ago we came across a fast-food operation with only about six or eight locations that we really liked. We talked to the owners about buying them out, partnering, or even paying them a piece of future earnings if we could build a company using their proven concept. We could have left them with ownership of the original stores and we would have owned the future stores, paying them a handsome royalty. They didn't have the passion, vision, or desire to take a good concept and prototype and turn it into a billion-dollar company. We loved the model and we had the vision along with the desire. They would not do it because they thought that someday they may want to expand themselves. Of course they have not to this date, and this was seven years ago. They could have made $100 million by now had they had the vision or the entrepreneurial spirit. I mention this because you may know of similar businesses. I am talking about small chain operations or single stores that have the potential to become large companies with hundreds of stores or concepts that will work in markets all over America. Buying a small operation that fits the bill for raising venture capital and eventually becoming a public company is certainly a possibility.

Do you know the McDonald's story? Well, one restaurant was how it all started. You do not have to be the inventor or creator of the concept to be the entrepreneur. I am always looking for the next big company, and you should be too. So whether it's your idea or concept, whether you buy it or build it, ask yourself how big it can be. Can this be a billion-dollar company? Do the math and see. If it can, then you are on your way.

two

Do the Math and See If It Works

In order to build the case that this idea, concept, product, or business can become a billion-dollar company we need numbers that prove it.

Our numbers or projections have to be for a minimum of three years but preferably five. Then you will have an understanding of the potential over a five-year period and what it will take to reach your billion-dollar level. You will most likely have to take the projections out even farther to get to the billion-dollar level in revenues. Once you have your rollout of stores or product up and running for three to four years you should be able to extrapolate out until you hit the billion-dollar mark. If you are selling a product you must have a solid sales model based on a sales plan that is believable and achievable. All your assumptions should be as accurate as possible since they will be challenged when you start raising money or trying to finance your business. You also want to make sure you do not kid yourself and believe numbers with bad underlying assumptions that can result in failure, loss of credibility, and possibly lots of money. When you start building your financial models you will want to ask a lot of questions and build your assumptions first.

Some of the questions you will need to ask may not have good answers at this point and you will have to make what we call "guesstimates." You can correct the models once you confirm the assumptions. In most cases you should not be far off if you know your business.

Before you build your models you will need to understand several things. Who are my customers? Where are my customers? How much will my customers buy? What will they pay for this product or service? What are my costs and expenses and, therefore, what will my profit margin be?

First, you need to understand your cost to build or produce the product or products. This is an essential step that so many people miss. It is more common to underestimate the expenses than to overstate the revenues. You may want to consult with an accountant to make sure you are not missing anything including insurance, taxes, license fees, and attorney costs. All of these things will need to be in the profit and loss numbers as well as on the balance sheet. You will need to properly expense all supplies and other usable items. Do not put out a set of numbers that has holes—do your best to make sure you are as accurate as possible.

Also remember that you will use the cash you raise to fund the expenses. Accuracy is important so you and your investors will not have any surprises. Your credibility is also very important in these early stages of building your company. It is likely that you will have to raise another round of cash, and you will need to be able to say, "Look at my track record."

What is the cost to operate a single store or the cost of operation? Remember, as I mentioned earlier, include everything so that you start out on the right track with the proper assumptions. There are many other assumptions you will need to make that will be specific to your business. Also you will need to build a cash flow and cash burn analysis. I am not an accountant, but I am including this basic information in the book for those who might need it. There are two types of accounting systems, cash and accrual. In most cases you will need to do all your profit and loss projections using the accrual method. Your accountant can help you set this up if you do not have an accounting background. Once you complete your three-year projections and your cash flow analysis, then complete your pro forma balance sheet based on your projections and cash flow. Once you fully understand your cash needs to start the business you can then do pro formas based on receiving that cash so the potential investor will understand the impact his or her investment will have on the company, whether or not the company will need another infusion of capital, and, if so, when.

Raising your money in stages is actually less costly then taking it all down at one time. In my first venture deal the money came in as we reached certain milestones. It is possible to structure your deal so that as you raise money over time and as the company's revenues and profits increase, the price goes up for the investor. The advantage is that you end up owning more of your company, therefore lessening dilution of your ownership.

For example, if you raised $1 million at $1 per share that would equal 1 million shares of your company. If you had 2 million shares outstanding, your investor would own 50 percent of your company. The investor would have valued your company at $2 million if the investor bought 50 percent of it for $1 million. Now if the investor put the money in as you needed it in stages, such as $500,000 at $1 per share, and when revenues reached predetermined achievable goals or other milestones, such as opening the office, hiring certain people, starting production, or something else you both agree on, then the investor would put in the next $500,000 at $2 per share or some price north of his first investment. The first $500,000 investment was priced at $1 per share, the company owners had 1 million shares, and so that would value the company at $1.5 million. At the next round let's say they issued 250,000 more shares at $2 per share so the company would now be valued at $3.5 million.

Let's do the calculations. When we sold 500,000 shares at $1 per share and we had only 1.5 million shares, then $1 × 1.5 million shares gave us a valuation of $1.5 million. When the investor paid $2 per share, $2 multiplied by our new number of shares of 750,000 to the investors and 1 million to the owners equaled $3.5 million. ($2 per share × 1.75 million = $3.5 million.) By simply waiting on the achievement of milestones before taking down the additional $500,000 we were able to increase our company's valuation by $1.5 million and reduce our dilution substantially. The investor is in at an average price of $1.50 versus $1 and only got 750,000 shares rather than the 1 million the investor would have received; therefore, you experience less dilution. The investor only has 42.8 percent of your company instead of the 50 percent the investor would have had if the investor had put all the money in up front at $1 per share and bought 1 million shares. Now you as the founder still have roughly 57 percent rather than 50 percent. This strongly makes the case for spreading the investment over time with milestones. The price increases to the investor because his risk goes down as the company achieves the milestones.

There was a time the markets were so volatile that the older and wiser guys told us young guys to take the money when you can get it regardless of the cost. This came from those who had experienced markets and times when you could not raise a dime. If that is the current situation then maybe you should throw the milestones out the window and take the money. You must get your dream financed if it is to become a reality. So use the "do what you've got to do" rule. We must realize that the cost of capital from the venture guys is the most expensive capital you will ever raise, and the milestone method of taking down the money will reduce your cost of capital substantially. If your company is a capital-intensive company then you may be forced to give up a big chunk of your ownership to get your dream off the ground or at least to the public markets where the cost of capital is much less and the investor is willing to pay much higher multiples of earnings.

If you are going the venture-capital route of raising money then you will need to build several financial models for raising that money showing the impact of different pricing and the use of various levels of cash. There are no absolutes as to how much you will be able to raise and what the price will be as there are many variables that will affect both the pricing and the amount of cash you will be able to raise. If you raise additional venture funds, you will continue with additional expensive dilution. However, this could be necessary if you are not quite ready to go to the public markets and you need money. Many times companies need what is called a "mezzanine" round of financing, and there are funds that prefer this level of venture financing versus the start-up investments. These funds are willing to pay a higher price, realizing that much of the risk of the business is gone and the company is about to reach a point of liquidity in the public markets. Sometimes the window for raising money closes due to bad market conditions, and companies just have to wait until the window opens up again. That forces them to raise another round of private-venture equity before they can get out with an initial public offering.

The venture capitalists want liquidity and they want big returns as soon as they can get them. They may be patient if they think they can get better returns, and some are more patient than others. The two routes of liquidity are simply the public markets or selling the company. If you do not want to sell your company then you will need to go the public market liquidity route or your life will most likely be miserable. The venture capital guys are some of the toughest, hardnosed business folks you will ever meet. They are smart and talented for the most part, and some of them who have been around for a while can bring more than their own money to the table.

They may have relationships with analysts or commercial and investment bankers as well as others who can bring value to you and your company. They can be a catalyst to your company's growth and success. Some of the more experienced ones can even bring credibility just because they invested in your company. The business world knows the tough due diligence that these firms perform on companies; they know that the venture capital firms do not just throw their money around, that they are smart investors, and when they put their stamp on you it says you are a grade A company and that they believe you are going places. Later we will discuss the venture capital business and how to position your business to raise venture capital.

Getting back to preparing your financial models, remember that you will want to include your general and administrative overhead, the costs of attorneys, accountants, human resources, and recruiting. Your investor will ask a lot of questions and you do not want to let the investor catch you leaving something out. If you have or will have some bank debt make sure all of the costs are included. Make sure your pro formas include cash flow models based on different growth rates and raising different levels of equity.

In the start-up company you will want to watch the use of cash very carefully. The venture guys will ask you constantly, "What is your cash burn rate?" and you will also want to know this daily because your cost of capital is so high you cannot waste any of these funds. I have seen so many chief executive officers of start-up companies forget that this is a temporary situation, that this is very expensive capital and that they should not waste a nickel. So many times costs just get out of control when there is money in the bank. So you waste it and there you are trying to raise money again. Remember this is expensive capital, and if you have not met your goals they will take another big piece of equity in your company and you will have little choice but to let them do it. So the lesson here is to make sure you do not burn up your cash before you are cash-flow positive or until you achieve your milestones or goals and you are ready to go to the public markets. If you do burn up your cash, then be prepared to give up more of the ownership of your company. This is a common mistake chief executive officers make when they get the venture money. Everyone wants the big salary and the perks, but this is not the time to get those things. I was on the board of a venture-backed company when the chief executive officer wanted the country club membership and the airplane as well. This was not the time for those expensive perks. You should wait till you get to the public markets where the cost of capital is much lower. By then the company should be cash-flow positive and profitable enough to afford these things if in fact they are needed and earned.

Once you complete your cash burn analysis it should encourage you to find ways to reduce your use of cash. You should be focused on how to produce sales and profits. Your number one goal has to be to breathe life into this company, and the best way to do this is to get the company on its own two feet and in the black. As you build your models you will want to build A, B, and C models, with A being your best and most profitable and the one you will want the investor to focus on. Each model should have different levels of sales and maybe even different services or whatever fits your business model. It may be that you have different models for different demographics. We see this in all types of businesses. For example, hotels, grocery stores, and even airlines operate differently in different-sized markets. So your projections and financial models may include a variety of different assumptions. Take a look at your growth plans. You know your area better than anyone. You may live in a big city where you can operate several A models and a couple of B and C models in the suburbs. There may be smaller cities in your expansion or growth plans where the B and C models will work well. In the B and C models the revenues will obviously be less and so will expenses and profits. But your start-up and fixed costs should be less as well.

Our goal is simply to try and lay out a plan that is realistic, even if it is not perfect, that will give us an understanding of what our numbers might look like under different scenarios. We will most likely find by laying out these projections what our game plan will need to be in terms of growth and expansion. For example, you will see the revenue and profit growth difference with the various combinations of models. You may need to do more A's than C's. We will cover the importance of branding your company in a later chapter. When you build a network of locations in a certain geographic area you begin to quickly brand your business. This allows the people in that area to become familiar with you. It also allows them to begin to recognize you as a company or a business where they can expect to get certain products or services and a certain level of quality. If you spread your locations out too far from each other you lose that quick branding opportunity and may increase your overhead and management expenses for that geographic area as well.

If your business is selling a product or a service through other business or retail outlets, your model will be different from the store models. When you own the stores you may need to use similar models. For example, let's say you are manufacturing a product or products like sunglasses or some type of jewelry that can be sold in retail stores. I am sure you will have your product in big stores where there is a lot of traffic or large population areas and you will most likely place your product or products in smaller markets and smaller stores as well. So in your demographic analysis determine how many stores could possibly sell your product or products. Project a conservative number with conservative sales in these stores.

Plan a rollout with marketing and advertising. If your conservative estimates and projections present a picture worth pursuing and you have tested your product or products for customer satisfaction, durability, safety, and quality while meeting all regulatory standards and requirements, go ahead and complete all your projections and pro formas to include start-up costs and cash burn rate. Do you have manufacturing established? Will you be the one to manufacture the product or products? Are you the distributor? In many cases serving as your own distributor is best and in some cases instead products are shipped from the manufacturing operation directly to the customer and you may never touch them.

This does require that you inspect quality and customer satisfaction on an ongoing basis. If you warehouse products and ship, you will have to make sure these costs are included. This discussion could go on for a while, but you understand that all things must be thought out well, all costs must be included in your projections, and the projections need to be real and achievable.

If you are making a presentation to potential investors your presentation might follow the outline below:

I. Introduction to the industry or business
II. Demographics of the business
III. Market size and opportunities
IV. Description of your business and brand
V. What makes you/your business different from others, including discussion of your competitors and why your company and product is better or different
VI. Your management team and their experience
VII. Financial projections with assumptions (Make sure you have cash flow projections. I would

provide a detailed three-year projection and maybe roll it out to five years.)

VIII. Your strategy and plan to achieve the financial goals

IX. How much money you plan to raise and how you plan to use it

X. Summary that includes the timing of funding and the reasons they should invest in your company

three

Where Do You Get the MONEY?

So now you have your numbers and you should have a good understanding of how much cash you need to get started building this business. How are you going to get the money? How are you going to value the company? How much money will you try to raise, and will you do it in stages? You have various options for finding money.

Here are your options:

1. Your own money
2. Friends and relatives
3. Companies that might have an interest in your industry, product, or business
4. Wealthy individuals who make start-up or venture investments, also known as angel investors
5. Venture capital firms or funds
6. Commercial banks
7. Public equity markets

Some people are fortunate enough to have the money to start their own businesses. When I started my first company I had just cashed out of a company merger where

I had made a few hundred thousand from the sale of my stock options. The money was burning a hole in my pocket, so I was glad to invest some of it into the founding of a new company. I believed in the vision and idea that I had, so I had no problem putting money into the deal. I was very excited about starting the new company, but I in no way knew at the time that I was starting a business that would become a multibillion-dollar company and that I would spend the next twenty years as the CEO and chairman. I was able to gather enough money to get the company doors open and to prove to the venture investor who put in the first round of venture money that we were going to build a company.

The commitment of our own funds is a very telling event to the investor. Seeing you willing to put your own money at risk makes it a little easier for the investor to join in and commit to invest and take the risk with you. Many times the investor will look at your financial situation to determine what a serious commitment might be for you. For example if you are worth $1 million, then a $50,000 investment might not be very much, whereas if you are worth $100,000 and you put in $50,000 you have made a serious commitment by putting up half of your net worth. Most of your venture folks will expect you to have some money in the deal. If you believe in what you are doing, you should want to buy as many founders' shares as you can. You would be buying your stock at a nickel or a dime per share and selling shares to the venture fund at a dollar or more a share depending on your valuation. Your shares are cheap because you are the visionary and it is your vision, abilities, and sweat that is providing the investor the opportunity to invest; that is why the founding shares are often referred to as "sweat equity."

Even if you do not personally have the money to fund the start-up of your new venture or business you may know people or have some friends or relatives who have money and they may be willing to invest in your dream. This would depend on your relationship with them as well as your history and how good you are at convincing them your dream is a wise investment. This can work well if you make them a lot of money, and if you do not, well, you may have trouble at the next family reunion or block party. These relationships still make a good place to get funds, and if you raise venture money they will all want to buy some cheap shares at that time. So if you have room and the venture guys let them in, you may want to sell them some shares. I have seen situations where the venture guys took all of the shares and refused to let anyone else in the deal. If you can raise enough money from friends and relatives to get the business off the ground, then your venture round, if needed, will be a lot less expensive.

In other words, if your company is up and running and has positive cash flow or it is getting close to cash flowing then the venture capitalists will have to pay much more for their shares. You start with a much higher valuation and therefore less dilution of your ownership and those who kick-started your business with their investment. So if you can get a jump start with money from family and friends and get the business down the road a bit before trying to raise venture capital, you should do it. If not, then the venture guys will get more of the company.

As I mentioned, some of the venture guys do not like relatives in the deal, but if you have a great concept and it is making money then they may not have a problem with it. They have more of a problem with nepotism than having family members as investors. Some venture guys will want to take the family members out of the deal, but that is not usually necessary.

Another source of funds can be companies that benefit from your business, supply your business, or in some way are in your industry. When I was the CEO of a large health-care company I made a lot of investments in other health-care companies, some that I thought had some vertical connection to our business and some that I just believed were good investments that we would get a good return from. We had incredible profits on most of the investments, and our overall return was impressive. So this may be another area you should pursue if it makes sense for your business or idea. Your valuation will most likely be higher than with the venture guys but certainly not any worse.

Now, we know that commercial banks will not lend you any money without assets, collateral, or cash flow to secure their loan. So if you are in a start-up mode with negative cash flow and no assets (or very little), do not expect commercial banks to acknowledge that you exist. If you are buying a business that has assets, is profitable, and does have cash flow that can support the loan then the banks may help you. Once your company reaches a certain level of profitability the banks will play a very valuable role in the life of your company. Commercial banks really do not do anything to help the start-up model or the young company trying to get its first traction. It is good to build a working relationship with the bank you use for your checking account and deposits so when the time comes you will be a known entity with a positive relationship.

When going to the venture guys first you better be ready for the beating of your life and the microscopic and thorough probing that you will have to endure. I must say that if they fund your dream, any pain you go through is worth it; however, once they are in they will stay very close to you until they are out. Your goal has to be to get the money and then get them to liquidity, which gets you to some liquidity as well. This gives you some peace and of course, makes you very wealthy. Some say it is not about the money, but believe me, it is always about the money. Just wait until you have a couple of venture capitalists on your board—it will always be about the money. If your company is to have life, it must be profitable. I cannot tell you how many chief executive officers I have known who lost sight of profitability and got focused on achieving other goals. If you do not take the company to profitability, then you will be raising money again and you will continue to give away ownership of the company. It is not easy to raise money. If you miss your profit goals and you have to raise money, you will suffer major dilution of your ownership. Sometimes companies have to raise money at less valuation than previous rounds, and that is very painful. This can also cause the board to begin to sweat, and some of the members may start to get uneasy and question whether or not you know how to get the company to profitability. It happens, and sometimes the CEO gets fired.

A lower valuation means that the venture capital firm has to lower the investment on its books, and they will see to it that you receive serious pain for doing this to the firm. Most of the time you will have the board weighted in your favor as a private company, but if the venture guys want someone to go and their continuing to finance the company requires it, then you have a difficult decision to make. That is why so much due diligence is required before a venture fund will finance a deal. The venture capital firms never want to be faced with having to fire the entrepreneur and the visionary. This is usually a disaster, and the company loses a lot of ground. This is why it is very important that you make sure your investors understand the good and the bad that can happen when building your business. Remember the outline in the previous chapter that you can use to present your PowerPoint' presentation to a venture firm or other investors. What would your PowerPoint look like? It has to hit all the points so the investor is fully informed about the company and business they will be investing in. The presentation should also let the investor know that you know your business and the industry your company is in.

So those are your options for raising money. Your approach to each of these options will be somewhat different. If you have the money to start your company yourself, you are in a small percentage of people. Building your own company is fun and exciting. Raising money is not always fun and can be the most difficult part of getting your business off the ground. Do not get discouraged if your business is truly worth financing. You will get it financed if you do not give up.

I have seen some mediocre businesses get financed. The CEO was convincing and passionate about his ideas and he obtained his financing because the investor believed in the entrepreneur and his passion. I have even heard investors say the concept was not that great, but "this guy is going to do something big; he is a winner." I have also seen the original concept change after the financial results did not come in as planned and the investor continued to finance, believing that the CEO and management team had the skills to build a successful company.

So before we fully discuss the approach to each of our capital sources we need to discuss building our management team so we can get financing.

When I first raised money the process was very strict and tough. Then as the tech bubble began to build in the '90s, venture money was thrown at a lot of management teams and concepts that were never able to earn the first dollar. Things were happening too fast. Ideas with management teams seemed to pop up everywhere, with teams explaining their concept wherever there was a pile of money, and, after giving their pitch, they would always say, "So do you get it?" The Internet was new, and its uses and potential were so unknown that the investor could imagine anything, so the investor would say, "Yeah, I get it." Otherwise the investor would look as if he or she did not understand or have the vision the presenting team had. No one would ever want anyone to think that he or she did not "get it."

Now, I never heard anyone ask what the heck "it" is. Investors were trying to make deals work; companies went public even though no one had a real understanding of the revenue model. Venture capitalists put money in deals because the idea man looked and sounded good. The venture guys thought they would figure it out because these guys were smart and they had worked for some good companies that had been successful in the past. They would say, "We need to do this deal before someone else does." Valuations made no sense. Valuations were sky high for companies that would never make one dollar in revenue. The management teams wasted money on plush corporate headquarters with nice logos, training rooms with a lot of computer technology and servers, along with nice desks, conference tables, chairs, security systems, phone systems, lots of administrative staff, accountants, and computer nerds hacking away all day every day without anyone ever knowing exactly what they did. It was necessary to have a lot of these guys. Their presence would guarantee you a couple more venture rounds. Well, all good things must come to an end, and when the tech bubble burst all that remained were companies with revenues and profits.

This, of course, is the way things should have been in the first place because this is the way the real world works and always will. At some point companies have to make a profit. The market gets hot and overpriced then the truth comes out and the leveling takes place. This means that the businesses that will never make a profit lose their investors as they head for the hills. As I reflect on all of this I remember a lot of bright young investors and entrepreneurs blowing smoke and making promises and believing in something that they could not explain in terms of real profitability and long-term sustainability. There were no old guys trying to convince other old guys or anyone of some great new virtual company that would spread through the world in a takeover attempt of whatever industry they might be conquering. The old guys kept saying one day these companies would have to make a profit, but none were bold enough to say it too loudly because as far as they knew maybe they "just didn't get it," and they didn't want anyone to know.

We have this thing on earth called gravity and that is why there are no "pies in the sky." Billions and billions were lost during this boondoggle of a time. I even lost a few million thinking that I "got it" or maybe that I "had it." Public companies were here one day and gone

the next. They would get a quick round of venture money and put together the management team then run to Wall Street to raise as much as the market would let them have, and, believe me, it was plenty. Most of them lost it all, and when the bubble burst and the money dried up so did the companies because they had no revenue or profits.

After this debacle, due diligence came back and investors started looking for cash flow and profits once more. They started asking the right questions again and began to check references on the management teams. Finally valuations got back in line with growth rates, revenues, and earnings and good solid deals started to flow again. You will have a loser slip through the cracks on occasion, but for the most part real companies are getting financed nowadays.

four

Building YOUR Management Team

The investor will be looking very closely at the CEO/
entrepreneur to see what kind of people he or she can
surround him- or herself with. What kind of talent can
this person attract? Does he or she have CEO leadership
skills? Will the person hire smart talented people who
may even be smarter than him or her? Does this person
recognize talent? If the person surrounds him- or herself with friends and family, he or she may have a much
harder time raising money. Even as a young company the
résumés of your management team will speak volumes
about you and the company's future. Your initial valuation from the venture capitalist (if you get financing)
will be higher if you have a talented management team
that has experience and has been involved in building a
company before or that at least has worked for a successful company. In other words, a team of people who have
done it before or at least were there so they know what
has to be done.

I remember when I did my first round of venture capital and I was asked for twenty references. Then the venture capitalist firm asked for almost as many references

from all the original members of the management team. The firm wanted references from my childhood all the way up to my current job.

You cannot build a billion-dollar company by yourself. You must have a team to build the business, and you must have a good management team before you can raise your money. The type of business you are in will drive the skills and educational background of your management team. However, there will always be a need for finance, sales, marketing, human resources, administrative support, operations, and possibly legal assistance. One of the first and biggest mistakes you can make that can prevent you from building a billion-dollar company is your management team selection. It may not matter how good your idea or concept is; if you cannot raise the money you are a nonstarter. If your team does not execute and get your company off the ground then you will fail. So your management team really is very important and may be the difference between success and failure.

What will your team look like? Remember that the venture capitalist will study the members of your team and inspect them very closely before investing in your company. Their résumés and qualifications will go under the microscope. Even one item that does not check out could cost you the deal. You will need to get your mind right as you begin your recruiting process. Here is the picture you need to keep in mind: as you recruit and hire you need to be thinking, "What will the venture capitalist or institutional investor on Wall Street say about my team?"

Questions you should ask yourself about each individual on your team:

- ❖ What is the person's appearance?
- ❖ Is it professional?
- ❖ How does the person present him- or herself?
- ❖ What does the person's rèsumè and bio look like?
- ❖ Does the person's education and skill set fit with the positions he or she has?
- ❖ What is the person's employment history?
- ❖ What will the person's references say?
- ❖ Can I say this person is proven?
- ❖ Has this person done it before?
- ❖ Why or why not would the investor put his money behind a team with this person on board?

As you hire your initial management team you need to keep these questions and issues in mind. How will these individuals do when interviewed by the investor, the venture capitalist, or the Wall Street fund manager? Your original top three to five executives will be the most important; the next layer will be a little less important in raising money but extremely essential in meeting your business goals. Family members work only rarely. It is usually better not to include family in top management because Wall Street does not like it. Sometimes the family member is carrying a heavy load or has a critical position and does a great job. Some very successful companies have been built by parent-child and sibling teams. Sometimes combining family and management turns the investor off. It can be a roll of the dice. Just know it is risky and that it can go either way.

Remember, you will be putting your team through a beauty contest every time you bring in a venture capitalist or sophisticated investor to consider investing. Once you become a public company the institutional investors constantly put your team through the beauty contest. If you have a great team you get a higher multiple when raising money. In other words, Wall Street pays more for a good team. They believe a strong team will outperform a weak team, and they should.

Who will be your inner circle? Jesus picked twelve to be His disciples but only three were in His inner circle. Remember one of the twelve turned on Him. Judas Iscariot was His treasurer and finance guy. He was not an honest man. This happened to Jesus and it can happen to you. You will have key people who will turn against you and may even cost you your business, money, productivity, and legal fees. I cannot emphasize enough that you must be very careful putting your founding management team together. It is absolutely essential that your inner circle be God-fearing, honest, and trustworthy people. I am not sure you can really ever know who people are. Money and power affect people differently. Someone who has always seemed like a wonderful, honest, hardworking person in his or her lifetime can become a real Frankenstein once the person is in a powerful high-paid position. Unfortunately I have experienced what some people will do when they get a taste of power and the big bucks.

There may also be fallout in the original management team you put in place. Some will certainly work hard and be loyal to the cause and company but not all. You will find that some people feel that you owe them a job and salary—this of course has been termed the entitlement syndrome. Some will take the job but will never perform in the position. They will never do the job you hired them to do. You need to be aware of this and stay on top of it. Once you see who is working and who is not, you need to give fair warnings and then do the surgery. Your goals and objectives must be clearly stated up front and in writing to each person on the team so you can surgically remove anyone who does not perform. This way there will not be any misunderstandings as to why the person was terminated. You just cannot have nonproductive people in a start-up company.

The best thing you can do is never hire anyone who is not on fire and passionate about helping you meet your goals and plans. Do not hire people you do not need. It is so easy to let your overhead slip up on you. Keep your overhead low during your start-up years. You should have one goal, and that is building your company's sales and revenues so that it gets to profitability and positive cash flow. Everyone on the payroll must be pulling the wagon and helping you achieve that goal. When hiring anyone make sure it is clear that the person will be working hard and productively to get you to that goal. This does not mean everyone has to be in sales, but it does mean that everyone has to do his or her job and carry as much of the load as possible.

Now, before you hire anyone to be in your inner circle or on your senior management team it is crucial that you interview the person several times. You will need to dig deep into who the person really is. Study everything each person has ever done in their life and why. You can learn a lot about a person if you not only study what he or she has done but also why. Does he or she wear the same suit or tie each time? What about shoes—are they shined? Is this person well groomed? What about attitude? Is it the same each time? Ask some of the same questions to see if you get the same answers every time. Did this person play sports? If he or she did not play sports ask why not. It does not mean that if someone didn't play sports he or she is not qualified for the job, but if this is going to be one of your top generals you need to know everything. If the person did play sports, how did he or she do? Is this person a winner? What if he or she says, "I'm really not very good at sports"? Is it a physical problem or lack of motivation? You do not need a passive person on your start-up team. You need fighters, people who will give it their all to win.

Build yourself a winning team that will strive to achieve your business goals. Successful businesses are competitive, and you need tough people who have a built-in competitive spirit, drive, and productive work ethic. If your competition beats you out of getting a business deal because your team was not strong enough to fight for the victory then you, by virtue of hiring them, have set yourself up never to be number one in your industry. Think about what I am screaming. You need to hire the best team you can and challenge them to be champions. You are the coach, so what kind of players do you want on the field? I recall once I hired a young man who had attended all the right schools and answered all the questions right in the interview but within one year he failed at everything we sent him to do. During your interviewing process when filling important positions dig deep as this was an expensive hire since we received no return on the investment in salary and training and we lost deals to competitors that would have generated substantial profits.

Another vitally important interviewing technique is to take anyone whom you are interviewing for your top management team out to dinner a couple of times. You should take him or her out once without the person's spouse and once with the spouse so you can see the difference in the personality alone and then with the spouse. Of course, you would only have the second dinner if the first dinner went well, all the reference checks were good, and you were seriously looking at hiring this person. During the first dinner you will find out if the right chemistry exists. I also want to see how this person acts in a fine-dining setting. How does the person order? What does he or she drink and how much? I have interviewed candidates who had too much to drink. You need to know this about the person you are recruiting. There is so much you can learn over a two-hour dinner. Make sure you include dessert and coffee if you want to extend the process.

This dinner sets up a situation for you to get a deeper look into who the person really is. If you are male and you are interviewing a female executive, take your spouse or another executive with you. If you are a female interviewing a man, then take your spouse or another executive with you. Now if this person does not fail the dinner interview and makes it to the next spousal dinner, you will get an even better look into this person. You will want to pay attention to how the spouse acts and, most of all, whether the couple has mutual respect for each other. There are a lot of things to observe in this valuable process.

During your dinner you will want to discuss politics as well as your business plans. Learn as much about the person's motivations and ideologies as you can. What hobbies does this person have and why? How about the children and family? Do not forget to talk about religion as well. As you are making this decision remember you may be making a twenty-plus-year decision and even a lifetime hiring decision. This is such a great opportunity and one of the most critical and tactical decisions you will make in the life of your company. Build yourself an all-star team that can take you all the way to the top!

Your attorney will also be a very important member of your management team; of course you will not need a full-time attorney when in your start-up mode. Your business will determine, in the long run, whether or not you will have a legal department with full-time legal counsel. You will also need an outside accounting firm, a commercial bank, and at some point an insurance agent to make sure you have all the proper coverage. Once the company is up and running and in the black you will most likely need an investment banker as well. Choosing these professionals is just as critical as choosing your management team. If you get bad or inferior advice from any of these advisors, it can have a serious effect on your ability to grow your business, meet your plans, or achieve your bottom line.

A bad attorney, when negotiating or trying to close a big or critical acquisition or business deal can kill the deal. You must select outside counsel that understands business transactions as well as venture capital and securities. You need someone who gives you all the right advice to help set up your company properly so you can raise capital privately or publicly. All your financing as well as all your contracts, both business and employment, must be done correctly. This law firm must have a good securities lawyer who can help with your corporate governance issues and organize your board committees and minutes. Do not underestimate any of these concerns. Remember, we are going to build a billion-dollar company and everything needs to be done properly and professionally.

During your start-up years, negotiate a discounted rate with your attorney. Good associates can help keep costs down, so interview the associates as well as the partner(s) you will be working with. The law firm will need to be willing to make an investment in the future by giving you some real haircuts on their rates during your start-up years until the company is profitable. Ask for at least 30 percent discount during your startup period. You will need a fairly senior person or partner at the firm who is your contact. This person is someone you will need to have good chemistry with and whom you can work well with. You will need to be able to talk to this person about a lot of things as your company grows, so hire someone you trust and who has a lot of wisdom and experience. In one of my companies I was fortunate to have just that person. I found an attorney that had been involved in venture capital deals, public offerings, and acquisitions. He understood how to structure the deals and he understood business. He and I would talk over all the deals that we did in the early days. We discussed the pros and cons of how each deal should be structured. He was really a great asset to our management team. If you are serious about building a billion dollar company find someone like the fellow I had. He was not only a great attorney he was a friend as well.

Your accounting firm will also play a very important part in your future. As the company gets bigger and bigger it will need a national or a recognized regional accounting firm that is acceptable to Wall Street to provide you with the proper audits and controls necessary to meet the corporate governance requirements of being a public company. You will also need a partner or very senior person at this firm to be your contact. Again, like the attorney, you will need someone you can discuss vital issues with as you grow and expand your company. Initially you will need to set up a good accounting department, and you will want this person to help make sure all the bases are covered. It is a good idea to ask the outside accounting firm to take a look at the associates at the accounting firm who will be working with you to make sure they meet your needs and requirements. Negotiate discounted fees with the accounting firm during your start-up period and until you are profitable. This firm will be doing your audits and presenting to your finance and audit committees of the board of directors, and they will need to make full board presentations as well. They will also present at your annual meetings of shareholders once you are public. If you have to fire your auditors, it can be looked upon as an indication of problems, so make sure you start with the right ones.

Once you are a public company I highly recommend that you make it a policy to rotate your auditors at least every four to five years at minimum—every two to three years is even better. This firm will be evaluating your business systems and controls and reporting to your board and shareholders about whether or not they are sufficient, so you should use them and get their input as you develop those systems and controls. Your accounting firm will also meet with your internal auditing people at least quarterly to ensure they are performing in a satisfactory manner. You want a strong accounting firm that will create financial reports that are always accurate. If the partner from the accounting firm is not pushing both his or her staff and yours to do a good job you will need to ask for another partner.

Good financial reports are vital to properly manage and run your business. The investment community expects you to have a skilled accounting firm doing your audits as well as advising you on controls, systems, and compliance issues. Your accountants will also play a large role in helping you prepare your public offering documents and all of your quarterly and annual SEC filings. Also, once you are public your acquisitions will trigger disclosure filings and reports, and your accountants will assist the attorneys in preparation of these filings. In a public company listed on the New York Stock Exchange the CEO cannot be a member of the audit committee meetings. The majority of the board members on this committee are required to have business, accounting, or finance backgrounds. The chairman must have the same.

The audit committee will meet with the accounting firm to discuss the quarterly earnings and to approve the earnings release. The accounting firm will discuss the annual audit, their plans for performing the audit, the resources they need, their timelines, and their management letter. Their management letter will inform the board in general how they feel about the management and their performance as well as the quality of the controls and the company's books, receivables, debt and anything else they may be concerned about. They will update the audit committee on controls, systems, compliance issues, and any problems or deficiencies. It is a good idea, as discussed earlier, to change your auditors on occasion to prevent them and your people from getting too comfortable with each other and to make sure no one gets lazy and overlooks anything. I would certainly worry if your financial leadership were classmates in college or if they played golf together on weekends. I am specifically talking about the auditors doing the work on the audit and your accounting people working with them. As you are building your company and your board of directors you will need to select individuals who can serve on this committee. Do not forget a business or accounting background is absolutely necessary.

Selecting your commercial banker is also a very important part of completing your management team. This can be a challenge, depending on where your business is based. It is nice to have a banker close to you and preferably in your home town. This is not always feasible. If you are in a big city, chances are you will have no problem finding a banker that can stay with you as you grow. Small-town banks are not set up to bank companies that grow outside of their communities. They usually do not participate in bank syndications, and if they do it is through their corporate headquarters or regional office. Remember, they also do not lend money to companies not making a profit or companies that are not cash-flow positive. The big regional banks usually have a corporate finance department or group within the bank that works with growing companies that are expanding geographically, and they sometimes lead large credit facilities—or at least participate with other banks in credit facilities—for companies in need of large loans or revolving credit lines. If you can find the closest large regional bank and meet with their corporate finance people even though you do not need them yet, you will get a feel for who they are and whether they have an interest in what you are doing. You will be back to see them, and you need to tell them that.

You learn as an entrepreneur that you must speak some things into existence. You can set your company's account up at that bank and do your daily banking with the closest branch to your office. You may even want to drop in and see the president of the bank when you visit the corporate finance guys just to get a feel for top management at the bank. I have found that in most cases a quick step into the bank president's office to meet him or her and say hello is not a problem if invited by a loan officer. Some of these banks also have an investment banking division. Meet with these folks as well because if you intend to build a large billion-dollar company, you will need an investment bank at some point to either help with your IPO or to assist you in other types of financings such as a bond offering or maybe some type of convertible debt.

Investment bankers are also in touch with acquisition opportunities, and they can assist you in mergers and public financings as well as the divestiture of your company when the time comes. Having these early contacts is healthy because they give you a taste of what is to come and they are also prophetic. If you are really a true entrepreneur, then you can make it happen if you can see it in your mind. So go for it and speak it and tell others where you are going and what you are going to do.

five

Mergers and Acquisitions

If you are going to grow your company into a billion-dollar business and do it in one decade, you most likely will need to make a few acquisitions. I know there are some companies that have had explosive growth and have grown to the billion-dollar level without making acquisitions, but that is not common. Most companies buy up their competition or they buy vertically along the continuum of their industry. A good example of the vertical growth would be an automobile company buying the business that makes some of the auto parts or a health-care services company buying a health-care product company that makes products they use.

We were able to grow one of the companies that I founded and built into a multibillion-dollar company vertically across the continuum of care. Our focus was on patients who started with imaging to determine if surgery was needed—if the imaging determined they did in fact need surgery then we provided the surgery center. After the surgery we would perform the physical therapy and rehabilitation to return the patient back to work, to school, or to play if he or she was an athlete. So we owned the diagnostic or imaging centers, the surgery centers, and the rehab centers. We even grew it further by adding surgical hospitals on one end and rehab hospitals on the other end of the continuum. In doing this we not only became the single source for care and treatment of our patients, we added billions in revenue and we didn't have to get out of our lane. We stayed the course of treating those patients who had certain needs. Many companies, on the other hand, will move outside of the vertical process and get into other lanes of business that attract a different customer. Many of your really large multibillion-dollar companies do just that over time to expand and to grow their earnings.

Take General Electric, for example. They make MRI machines, appliances, jet engines, and many other products and they sell to lots of different customers. Yamaha is another company that is very diversified. They make motorcycles, guitars, wave runners, outboard motors for boats, just to mention a few. They have a broad customer base, but they have capitalized on their name. They have an excellent brand, so when they put their name on a product you expect and receive a level of quality. I have never been let down with any Yamaha product that I have purchased.

I talk about these companies because as you build yours you will make decisions about acquisitions and be faced with some that will be outside of your original business plan and have a different customer base. My advice is to stay your course until your original plan is achieved and is a mature business. I do not mean that your business has stopped growing but that you are well on your way to becoming a leader in your industry if not *the* leader before you start getting into other lines of business that have a completely different customer base. If you can keep your focus and put all your energy and thrust into your primary business, you will have a much better chance of being successful at building a strong business that can become a leader in its industry. When that business starts to mature and slow and you have reached your billion-dollar goal it may be time for you to look for opportunities to diversify the company's assets and earnings. This is not something you need to do while you are still a growth company. You may very well be in a business where you want to buy up or roll up your competitors. Wall Street seems to reward the pure plays with higher multiples, at least early on in the company's growth, giving the company a higher stock price and higher valuation.

Growing through acquisitions or rolling up others in your industry is a natural process and a great strategy to build a billion-dollar company. In the last ten to twenty years we have seen the banking industry begin a consolidation that has taken out most all of the regional banks. In this process some of the large regional banks have become national banks and the larger national banks mega banks, although our choices of banks as customers have shrunk. However, in Houston where I live, we are seeing the start-up of several small banks, and it will be interesting to see if they remain independent or if the big banks eventually buy them up. This of course is a good strategy for the founders of those small banks, as there is an opportunity for them to make a nice return if they sell to one of the big boys. Another industry where we have seen consolidation occur has been in food service. National chains of restaurants have acquired other regional chains. In these rollups they have kept the brand, invested money in expanding the brands, and in some situations they have put two different fast-food restaurants in the same building. This is a smart way to promote both brands, give the customer a choice while keeping the cost to the customer down by housing them in one building, and sharing in the overhead and using the same staff to serve. I believe the plan here was to drive twice as many customers through a single location by offering both products. If they were in two buildings across the street from each other you would have the same number of customers but double the overhead cost of delivering the products to the customers.

These are examples of consolidations or roll ups that have synergies that make sense and can be very accretive to your earnings. We have seen hotel chains buy other hotel chains and even car manufacturing companies buy other car makers. I believe that while you are still in your start-up years you need to stay in your lane and focus on building your profit and a good foundation of business that other companies may want to be part of one day.

Remember the stock market will reward you for staying a pure play by giving you a higher multiple, which puts you in a better position to make acquisitions and gives you a higher market capitalization or valuation. The reason for the higher valuation is the fact that you are focused on the single business. You should be able to grow that single line of business at a faster pace than others, and that gives you a higher growth rate and a chance to become the market leader. Now let's change the subject a little.

To whom would you want to sell your company? If you really build this business into a sizeable enterprise you will one day be thinking about liquidity. When you do, what kind of company will you be looking for to merge into or to be bought by? You will want a quality company with an impressive business model that has been a winner on Wall Street. Something that you believe will continue to go up in value because it has good leadership and a good track record. You will not want to park your shareholders into a company that is risky and that could go south soon after you join them. Build the kind of company that you would want to buy. If you get off track and out of your lane too early, you will most likely never make it to the industry-leader position nor will you be an attractive merger partner. I tell you this as a warning: if you really want to build value into your brand and your company's equity, do it right by following my recommendation above, then others will want to join you in time.

This brings us to another area you will need to understand, the area of mergers and acquisitions. Everything that you do as you build your company prepares you for truly building a billion-dollar business. What I mean is that the way you structure—from the beginning—the company with its funding, the management team, and the board will all play into what you will ultimately be able to become. Now I know that that is a broad statement, but let me explain and break it down so that you fully understand. If you build a management team that does not show and perform well, you are not going to be a darling on Wall Street that other companies will want to join. If your board of directors is just a bunch of your buddies and not successful business leaders who have done it before, then you may be hurting yourself again. If your financing is some hybrid structure that includes multiple levels of controls and different series of stock that no one can understand this could be detrimental. If you get out of your lane too early and buy some other business that does not fit with your primary company and you cannot explain any kind of vertical integration, you may be hurting yourself with that as well. I am simply saying that you will be in competition with other companies for shareholders and mergers and acquisitions candidates. How are you going to look when compared to other companies in your industry and on Wall Street?

If you put individuals on your board who do not have the experience or background to give you good advice and counsel, then you may find yourself in a battle with certain board members over important decisions. I had a board member at one company who gave me horrible advice. He had old-school success and was influential with other members of the board. They wanted to go with me, but I always had him as a doubting Thomas and it made my life miserable. Today as I look back at the things he advised us to do I realize how wrong he was. Things change and industries change and that board member's old-school mentality actually hurt our decision-making process and ultimately reduced the company's growth. We all know that hindsight is twenty-twenty, so we just have to move on and put it behind us as another lesson in life and business. I think I could write an entire chapter on some of the things this board member did and advised us to do. At the time he appeared to be somewhat on target, but now it is easy to see that he was completely wrong. You cannot trade anything for experience, and now I understand and can easily see the things we should have done that he kept us from doing. Knowing what I know today I would never have allowed him to influence the board the way he did and that company's history would read very different. A narrow-minded decision maker on your board can be a problem if you intend to build a substantial multibillion-dollar business. This is why you must have a good board that will look into the future and not just talk about how it has been done in the past. Finding a board member that has done something innovative in business is not easy but they are out there. Keep looking for someone who has vision and can see into the future so you will not only have that person there to back up your innovative thinking but this person will add value with his or her own ideas.

In order for you to understand where you need to take your company you must take the time to study other industries and look at the leaders in those industries. Pull all their financials and track the growth of the stock and their earnings and the price-to-earnings ratio or P/E ratio. You will see that some companies trade at a higher P/E ratio than others in the same industry. There are reasons for that, and you need to become a student of why that occurs. That will prepare you for what you need to do. The industry leader will almost always be the one with the highest multiple or P/E ratio. The reason is because

Wall Street speaks with their feet. If they are buying your stock more than your competition then your multiple will rise above the others. Wow! What a great revelation. Build your company so that it will trade at a higher multiple than your competitors. Do everything the right way so that they have to own your stock if they are going to invest in your industry. This concept is so important that it bears repeating: having the highest multiple in your industry, or at least one of the highest, will give you an edge and an advantage in buying other companies or doing a roll up of businesses in your industry.

It becomes simple math. You can pay more if you are trading at a higher multiple of earnings. The higher the multiple the more accretive the deal will be to you. For example, if your company trades at twenty times earnings and your next best competitor trades at sixteen times earnings then you can buy the company in play at a higher price because you will get a higher value for the earnings of the company you are acquiring. You can pay a higher price and the acquisition will still be additive or accretive to your earnings. This is so significant because you are now the front runner and most attractive company to merge with or to be acquired by. Companies that want to join with another will search you out or have their investment bankers contact you to see if you have an interest in buying them and at what price you might pay. They too can do the math and see who can pay the highest price. I guarantee they will do those calculations over and over if they are thinking of cashing out at some point. The investment bankers will constantly remind them of all of their options. If your investment banker is not constantly keeping you abreast of opportunities for buying and selling other companies in your industry then you need to change bankers.

I have to give credit to two of the best bankers in this country for making sure that I was always on top of my industry and business as far as opportunities. I will just leave it at "Ben and Bill"; those who were active in the health-care industry during the years I was rolling up companies will know who I am talking about. These guys were on top of the industry we were in. They kept us informed of everything that was happening so we could be positioned to move quickly when a company went into play. They analyzed every opportunity daily and would call us and tell us which companies we needed to be watching. They were on top of the markets as well. They made sure we knew when we needed to be preparing to go to the markets for debt or equity. They could smell a deal months before it ever happened. Another reason you must have a good investment banking team that truly will support you. Listen to their advice. I found them to be a tremendous asset to our team. Build a strong relationship with them and be loyal to them so they will do the same to you.

You will need to buy or sell at some point. One thing you can bet on is that things will change, companies will merge, companies will sell, and industries will consolidate. You will build a company that will fit into this monopoly system somewhere. The big question is where? Again, all this depends on how you build your company, and it begins at square one. Everything you do is important. You can make a few mistakes, but they cannot be critical ones.

We've already discussed many of the potential pitfalls. Other things that you can do to increase your valuation are to keep your overhead low and maintain a good growth rate as well. Your growth rate and your margins will play a major role in attracting investors. Valuation is directly proportional to the number of shareholders that you have and the volume of stock they buy. Well, if that is the case what can you do to make your company attractive to investors? That's what I keep trying to make sure you understand as you read this book. *Do the things that will make investors buy lots of your stock and want to hold it because they believe you will continue to build value into your company by making good, sound business decisions.* We all know that we do not live in a perfect world and there will be ups and downs, but if you have built a good foundation with a good base of business then when you do make a mistake or you have a shortfall or a bad quarter your strong base of business will carry you through the valley.

When you are at the top and you are the entrepreneur, the visionary, the leader, and decision maker you constantly evaluate your options. Thoughts go through your mind daily as to what the future will hold for your company. You want to make the right decisions. It is truly driven by the visionary's ability to see the future. When the vision has come to an end I believe it is time to do something different. If you can't come up with a new vision for the company to propel it into the future it may be time to sell or merge with another company. You always want to have a soft landing. Do not drive it into the ditch; instead place it somewhere nicely into a larger company, and that will make all of your shareholders happy.

I have found that many entrepreneurs who build companies want to get out at the point when they realize they may never become the industry leader, but not all will feel that way. Some will stay in for the long run and be happy just slowly building a good solid company and being number two, three, or four in their industry. However, many others will look to cash out and move on with their lives. The dream of getting out from under the pressure of Wall Street and the constant competitive pressure to grow the business is something that will work in your favor when you reach a point that your company is in a position to start buying other companies. I found the older guys the easiest to talk into a deal. I wanted to acquire their company and they wanted me to acquire it as well. They didn't want to admit it, but sometimes they wanted out so bad you could see the excitement in their eyes as they worked out the details of their non-compete agreement. It was usually a matter of respect and pride as to the price and structure of the deal. They didn't want to disappoint their shareholders and let them down. However, they all wanted to make sure they were taken care of too.

It is hard to give up the perks that come along with being the CEO of a nice-size public company. The big salary and bonuses that give CEOs the lifestyle they get accustomed to is one thing, and then if they have a corporate jet or plane you will have to deal with that as well. The problem here is that not only do CEOs get used to the luxury of a jet or plane but so do their families, and CEOs will fight for the right to have some continued use of that benefit. It is something that I always gave them because although it was not a big deal to us it was always a big deal to them. The perk of the plane was kind of like being on drugs and you just had to wean them off of it over time.

Sometimes in the larger deals you will have to put either the CEO or the chairman on your board for a few years or at least one term. This gives the shareholders who have to vote on doing this deal some assurances that someone will be looking out for their interest now that they will hold shares of the new company in exchange for their old shares. If it is a cash deal, however, then there will not be any board seats or airplane deals. They get the cash and you get the business. You may want to do some kind of earn out in cash deals along with non-compete agreements to make sure your new purchase does not evaporate after you buy it. I like the stock deals because they now have a vested interest in the success of your company, at least until they are able to sell all of the stock you gave them for their company. That will take some time; meanwhile they will be a cheerleader for you and your management team. They will most likely not go back out and try and compete with you again. Most of those chief executive officers will retire or do something else that they had always wanted to do.

Sometimes the problem for an outgoing CEO is giving up control, and you will see that a lot. There is a way to deal with that. The best way is to put the CEO on your board and treat him or her as if the person still has a voice. Let the person chair a committee and keep the person on salary and stock options. You can name him or her as a special advisor to the chairman and pay the person extra for that. All of these things will help him or her let go of the reins. This surgery is sometimes the hardest part of doing the acquisition. Many times that CEO is listening to someone who is telling him or her not to give up the ship, and, believe me, I have had that problem many times. It can come from parents, the spouse, good friends, other board members, or even the management who may be afraid of losing their jobs. Once you reach a deal you will have to hold the hand of that person until the deal is closed. So many times I saw CEOs get cold feet and I had to spend time with them reminding them how good the deal was going to be. I could tell when they had people whispering in their ears.

Do not ever think that just because you have a signed deal that it will happen. That is just the beginning. If the CEO wants out of the deal, he or she will find a way out as the due diligence process unfolds. A lot of times companies will include crown jewel clauses in the agreements to make sure that if one of the companies pulls out of the deal that company will have to pay a large penalty by selling one of their nice properties or paying a big cash bonus. This process takes some major leadership and salesmanship as well as some psychology. Over time you learn all the buttons to push when dealing with these very aggressive personalities who are also very smart people.

You may want to be one of the companies that is acquired, which is a good option as well. I know of many chief executive officers who had that intention when they started the company. There is nothing wrong with that, but you will still need to follow my advice in terms of building a quality company that will bring a premium to both you and your shareholders. If your management team is really good the acquiring company will want to keep them and they will also play a major role in helping you get a better price. Of course your company will be more profitable and have a higher valuation if built properly.

I love the roll-up model of building the billion-dollar company because it is faster, fun, and exciting. I promise you there will never be a boring or routine day once you start the roll up process. If you are in an industry where a roll up is possible then you will find out as I did. You begin to buy regional companies and before long you have a national company. There is no doubt being a national company helps you in buying other companies.

The big challenge will be managing it all. Doing the due diligence is critical because you do not want a company to slip something by you that will cost you in the long run. If their earnings are not what they say they are then you have to reduce the price accordingly. You will need language in the signed purchase agreement that allows for the price reduction if you find shortfalls in the earnings they gave you and that you used to price the deal. I was once in the middle of a $900 million deal when we found a shortfall of over $25 million in earnings. When we brought this to the attention of the CEO he would not adjust the purchase price and we couldn't go forward because the deal was no longer accretive to earnings. We could not do a dilutive deal because Wall Street would have killed us. The deal was not directly in our lane, but it was somewhat on the vertical continuum. It was a little tricky to sell anyway, and if it was not accretive we were afraid we could not sell it so we let it go. It was a sad day because it would have been a great deal at the right price. Make sure that you have a good due diligence team and that your future projections are achievable for those acquisitions and merger candidates.

As you add the companies and grow the business you will need to build a management team that has the depth to properly manage the businesses you are acquiring. Earlier in the book I talked about your attorneys and accountants as well as your investment bankers. When you start to grow through mergers and acquisitions you will be glad that you put together a good-quality team of professionals to help you operate in a quality way. You do not want to end up with shortfalls in earnings because of bad due diligence, and you definitely do not need to end up in lawsuits because of bad legal work.

In summary, I would recommend that you spend some time studying other growth companies that grew by acquisition as well as those that had explosive growth due to a great product or business.

six

Things That Can Go Wrong

I think sometimes our success may be the cause of our failures. It may be that the more successful we are the more we begin to make mistakes. Just think about it for a moment. When we are doing great it is easy to think, "I am doing all the right things." Of course that is when we start thinking, "Boy, I have got all this moving in the right direction, I have it all under control, and I am doing great." That is also when we are most likely to take our eyes off the road and end up in a ditch. Some of my trouble really began when I thought I had reached the point that I could relax and maybe kick back and move to the beach, buy the boat I had always dreamed of, and enjoy the benefits of twenty years of hard work.

What I would like to do in this chapter is to focus on how you, as the founder and CEO, can make sure that your company never has a major financial reporting problem. There is some good news in the public-company arena as governance requirements are in place to help avoid a lot of problems that can creep into companies, but it is not foolproof. Changing auditors and making sure that your audit and compliance committees are fully independent will solve a lot of problems. I went through a difficult time with one of the companies I founded and had spent twenty years building. These problems would never have happened if just one person had contacted our 1-800-FRAUD hotline and reported exactly what the CFO was doing when he created inaccurate financial reports. It would have stopped this activity and made the compliance committee of the board aware of what he was doing. The question is why someone in the financial department who was involved in preparing the numbers did not make the call. The calls were handled by an outside firm and they were totally anonymous, so no one would ever have known who made the call. I really struggle with why no one called and reported that the CFO was doing something wrong. If they thought I was doing something wrong as the CEO they should have reported me. There was lots of interaction between the financial team, the auditors and the audit committee of the board of directors. This alone created lots of opportunity for them to discuss any problems they may have had with any of the financial reports. Not one of them took the opportunity to report anything. I personally produced videos that went out to all employees discussing how to report any fraudulent activity within the company. I even spoke at management meetings telling all of our leadership that they had a responsibility to report any improper activity they were aware of. It apparently was not enough as no one reported the improper actions of the CFO and his team.

It is absolutely essential to properly train and direct your people to always report wrongdoings using the proper channels that the company has in place to deal with improper or illegal activity. Then it can be dealt with as soon as it happens, those involved will be disciplined immediately, and the situation can be corrected and dealt with without damaging the company. So when we look at things that can go wrong, not only can you find people at high levels who may do things that are wrong, but you may find a lot of improper things going on at lower levels as well. One of the companies that I had the opportunity to consult with had dozens and dozens of people stealing thousands of dollars from the company.

The first few months I was consulting with them they uncovered at least one to two people each week involved in some kind of theft. The thefts ran from several hundred dollars to as much as $30,000 to $40,000. I was shocked that we caught someone almost every week for the first few months. They were stealing from petty cash, they were stealing product, and they were writing fraudulent checks. It is a fact that those with the entitlement syndrome tend to believe if it belongs to the company it belongs to them. People take home office supplies, they cheat on expense reports, and they lie about overtime, and so on. Does this make all of these people criminals? Where do you draw the line? Certainly cooking the books is not acceptable at any time. But you need to be aware that even some of the best employees may do things that damage the company.

You must always be on guard and make sure you have systems and controls in place that will bring these things to your attention when they happen. You do not want to spend twenty years of your life building a great company to find out you have people working for you who are doing unacceptable things that could cost you your entire life's work. I believe once you are a public company you must also consider changing your CFO and controller every few years. I do not mean you must fire them but rotate them into different positions so that others can take a look at the decisions they have been making. I think when they know others will be looking at their work; they will be less likely to do anything improper. A CFO must have multiple skills and can be used in the mergers and acquisition area as well as planning and budgeting. Some may also have the leadership and management skills to run divisions of the company and that will help develop them into a CEO or COO for the future. There is nothing wrong with moving finance people around to make sure you never have a problem with the quality of your numbers. There are some that will disagree with me on this one, but if they had walked the same road as I they would understand my perspective.

If your company is a start-up trying to get financed this is not a current concern of yours, but it is something that I have to bring into the discussion at some point—and this is as good a place as any. Do not let your success lull you into a place where things can go wrong or slip by you that may have negative financial impact on the company. Somehow, for as long as you continue to sit at the top of the company as the chairman or CEO, you must keep both eyes on the road and make sure your company stays a winner. Not only can things go wrong internally, but most industries are very competitive. Your competitors would love for you to go to sleep at the wheel and give them an opportunity to take market share from you. Again, as a growth company kicking down doors and taking names you may not be thinking about these things at this time, but it is something that you will deal with over time if you build a large successful company.

Other areas in which you need to protect yourself include labor laws and various regulations that may apply to your business. Even as a start-up you want to pay close attention to labor laws, human resource and personnel issues, and regulations governing your industry so you do not run into problems that will slow you down or detract you from your goals. Pay attention to details so as to avoid getting into legal disputes or lawsuits that will cost you lots of money and time. There are companies that get caught up in lawsuits that cause them to burn up the venture money they raised to build the company. Remember, these funds are very expensive, and you gave up equity or ownership of your company to get them. The lawsuits will keep you from hiring people, building your business, and raising additional funds to keep the company growing. Just do not let yourself get into deals that end up in litigation. We live in a highly litigious society. Make sure you check all references on your employees and do not hire people who have a record of litigating previous employers. Setting your company up right from the beginning with a good accounting and a law firm with securities expertise will help you get started on the right track for building a successful company and business.

seven

Taking It to the Top

This chapter will give you some things to think about that may really make the difference between building an average company that never becomes an industry leader versus building a company that does become recognized as an industry leader. As we discussed previously the industry leader usually trades at a higher multiple of earnings than others in the same business, and there are real benefits to that. The higher multiple gives you an advantage when doing mergers or acquisitions using the company stock as currency. Having the higher multiple will allow you to make acquisitions that others with the lower multiple cannot. The reason is that those acquisitions will be accretive to your earnings and may be dilutive to theirs, which allows the company that trades at the higher multiple of earnings to make acquisitions that others cannot. Also companies that are willing to be rolled up into larger companies usually prefer to go with the winner or the industry leader.

You Make the Difference

There is a reason some companies become the industry leader and others do not. Do you know what makes the difference? Well, guess what, my friend? YOU make the difference! You as the leader, the coach, the visionary, the CEO, the boss, the one with the plan, and the one everyone expects to set the tone that will control the velocity at which you will grow. The management style and the team's work ethic, how hard the individuals on your team are going to work, in addition to your own efforts to build this company—are in your hands. You are the one at the helm, at the controls, driving the train, the truck, and the bus. You will decide who is on the board, the senior management, the junior management, the marketing and sales strategy, expense controls, culture, esprit de corps, and so on.

If you drive an expensive exotic car and make the company pay for it, then you will see others wasting time at the water fountain and in the coffee room talking about how you waste the company's money. Next, you will be faced with having to give your good people raises so they can buy nicer cars and bigger houses. Believe me; I know all about this as I once walked down that narrow-minded road. I personally did some things that caused conversation at the water fountain. Lots of your people will work very hard for you but they may never make the kind of money you make. Don't rub it in their face. Lots of CEO's make the mistake of doing that and it does not do you any good.

Just wait until you are a leader in your industry, the company is making incredible numbers, and Wall Street begins to fall in love with you before you start showing your wealth. I remember the Sam Walton story of how he continued to drive his old pickup truck and how he flew around in his little single-engine Bonanza even when he was one of the richest men in America. Warren Buffett did some similar things. I am telling you this because if I had to do it over I would do it differently. I guess now that I am a little older I am a little wiser and I see the real benefit of being austere when you are the leader of the company. Keep your overhead low and do the same with the company and you will not regret it.

You should know that your purchasing habits do set a tone. I was working late one evening at a company I was consulting with and the CEO drove up in his Lamborghini, gunning the engine as all the top management stood there. The team had been working late because the CEO had just reorganized the management with layoffs and salary reductions. Believe me, that was some really bad timing. After he left everyone was really upset with him. It was a horrible time to show off the fancy car. I am sure that some of the guys still talk about that moment to this day. You just have to use some common sense about things once you find yourself making the millions.

So remember that you are the leader twenty-four/seven in all you do and wherever you go, and everything you do will be exaggerated many times over. There may even be urban legends, stories that are not true, but no one will believe they are untrue because naysayers love to tell the stories. Do not give them any more fuel for gossip than you have to.

So how are you going to set the tone in your company as far as work ethic? Will you run a nine-to-five operation? Will you require some weekend work? What will your hours be? You will have to be there setting the tone and working late if you expect others to do it as well.

Don't Burn Through Your Seed Money

Once you get your venture money or seed money the race is on, and the fire has begun. The day you put the money in the bank you light a match to it. It is burning by the day, the hour, and the minute. What are you getting out of that seed money? Your personal equity stake in the company will be determined by how fast that money burns up or by how long it lasts—basically how much you can get done on the watch of that seed money. Remember, the next round you give up more equity. The more you have accomplished on that money the less equity you have to give up. Wow! Now have this revelation with me: this means that I must hire highly talented people who can close deals, increase sales and get things done fast, they must initially be willing to work hard for less pay, and they must understand that we are going to get up early and go to bed late until we stop burning money.

Once the company is cash-flow positive you can take some time off and maybe reward those who help you get there, but remember that the race never stops and you never get to quit as long as you are the CEO. It is always on you and with you. You can never stop pushing and pulling the wagon or making sure the board and the shareholders are happy—or, most of all, that you are happy with your accomplishments and the fact that you are a winner and are going to be a leader in your industry. This attitude will build you a billion-dollar company, which is what this book is all about. A lot of people can build a small business, but only a few will build the billion-dollar ones. You can do it, but you have to be driven and you have to really want it. You have to work smart and be alert, always looking for the next deal and the next opportunity.

I never stopped to take the time to celebrate the victories. We would close the new deal and get up the next morning looking for another one. I remember an investment banker wanting us to go on a trip to Italy to celebrate a big deal we'd completed. In my opinion it was a waste of time and money. We did let him buy us dinner and an expensive bottle of wine the next time we were in New York.

So the work ethic, the people you hire, and the way you spend the company's money is the basis for what kind of company you will end up with. I mentioned in an earlier chapter that some chief executive officers want to spend the venture money or seed money on perks. This is really something that you must not do. You have to spend those funds in a way that generates profits and cash flow. Some chief executive officers want to hire too many people, friends and relatives, and this is always a train wreck. Focus on the burn rate and how you are going to make this company cash-flow positive and profitable. Do smart deals that will bring in cash quickly, not long-term deals that will take a couple of years before producing results. Unless you are a high-tech company that will spend millions in research and development, you really need to hear what I am saying.

Actively Manage Your Team's Productivity

You will find once you begin to build your workforce and as the number of employees goes up the average level of productivity goes down. This is always true. There are also people who are experts at looking like they are working when they are doing very little to move the wagon up the hill. You as the CEO will always have to look for and motivate these people to be productive. The only way to find out who is in that category is to make them give you activity reports and have them tell you what they are doing by the day. In other words ask them, "What did you do last week and what are you going to do this week?" Get it in a report but also have meetings where you ask them these questions in person. This way you will know who is working and who is not. Once you have accumulated five or six reports you will be able to verify if they are doing the things they say they are doing. Sometimes you will find they will take credit for work others are doing.

To give you an example, I was in a meeting with the management of a company once and one of our mangers told me he was flying across the country to have a meeting with a doctor. I asked him why he would burn up two to three days as well as the cost of flying across the country to have a meeting with one doctor. I told him to come to my office and I would call the doctor to make sure we had a deal before we wasted the time and money. He was not even sure that the doctor would do business with us. I also told him he would need to set up additional meetings with other doctors in that area that we could do business with if he was going to make that trip. I wanted to be sure he was productive and the money was not wasted.

Monitoring of productivity and expenses is so critical when you are in start-up mode. Your people will waste your money and your time if you are not setting the tone to prevent it. Remember, some will try to ride in the wagon and others will even try and pull the wagon back down the hill. In large companies it is easy for someone to get into a management job and do very little real work as far as contributing to the building of the company. Some people can do it for years and even retire with the company having never really contributed to its success. Some will talk a good game and process lots of paper. These employees, when asked to travel for the company, will always be the first to turn in their expense reports. Hold everyone accountable for doing something that will contribute to the bottom line and profitability. Document their contributions in their performance reviews but also document their lack of contribution as well. It is particularly important to do this in your start-up years.

Your Product: The Best in the Industry

Now let's talk about your product. It should be the best in the industry. If it is not, you will have to make it the best. Do whatever you have to do to achieve that goal. In one company I was building we had over two thousand locations, and I wanted all the floors to shine and the facilities to be pristine. I believed it would make a difference to our customers. I had experienced dirty restrooms in businesses and dirty fast-food restaurants and I knew how it made me feel; I didn't want our customers to have that same feeling after visiting one of our facilities. We found out what we needed to do to have the shiniest floors and the cleanest facilities in the business. We then implemented what we called our "pristine program" throughout all of our facilities, and that program set high standards and expectations for everyone.

We also set up an auditing program where we checked to see if the program was being implemented, and this forced all facilities managers to fully implement all the standards, which in turn increased the quality of experience that each customer had while visiting one of our facilities. Afterward I started receiving letters all the time from our customers telling me how clean and wonderful our facilities were. This increased the professionalism of the employees as well as the productivity. Everyone took pride in our facilities. The question is, are you going to be the best in your business? If you want to build a billion-dollar company you need to give everything you have to make it the best. This is something you can decide to do and actually achieve.

Make Things Happen

How are you going to brand and market your product or business? I had a very smart investment banker tell me once that you have to have a good logo. He was so right. A good *logo* for branding purposes and a good marketing and sales plan is vital. *Another* thing you MUST remember as the CEO is that you are the number one salesman in the company. I cannot even begin to tell you how many deals I personally had to close out of the hundreds that I have been involved in. Sometimes it would take just a phone call to the person who made the decision, and sometimes it required me to actually make the presentation myself. Sometimes you need to have dinner or go deep-sea fishing or hunting with the decision maker. You just have to do whatever it takes to close the deal.

Remember, time is money and you are burning money every minute of the day. You will find that even when your company reaches a billion in sales you will still have to go and close deals and make things happen. The decision makers in the companies that you are buying and the deals that you are doing will expect to be courted. They will want to know who the leader is and what he or she is like. They will also want to feel as if you care about what is important to them. Your involvement in this area will be critical to your success and growth.

Do You Have What it Takes?

So now you are a salesman and director of marketing and branding. You are head of human resources, you are the money raiser, the strategist, the organizer of the board, the communicator to shareholders and Wall Street, and you are the product manager and the head of materials management. You are totally and completely responsible for it all, all the time. Are you sure you want to do this?

I was speaking to a group of very bright college students at Oklahoma State University, and I asked for a show of hands of those who would want to be one of the highest-paid chief executive officers in America. There were several students who didn't raise their hands, so I asked some of them why. They responded that they didn't want the responsibility or the risk. Well, if you do not want those things you really do not have what it takes to be an entrepreneur because the real entrepreneur does not even think about the risk. The entrepreneur is so driven by his or her vision and the desire to build his or her dream that risk and responsibility are the last things he or she would think about. It is the passion and the burning desire to build what the person has already seen in his or her mind or dream that keep the entrepreneur going. The entrepreneur knows it can become a reality because he or she has already seen it.

I hope that this book will help those entrepreneurs who have not built companies before achieve their goals with fewer difficulties than I had. I have included some real-life stories and real events that I hope will help guide the visionary to build his or her company into a billion-dollar business. Staying on top of your business and your industry and leading your troops to the goal line is what one must do to be successful. I cannot really put enough emphasis on how important it is to create a work environment and culture that bleeds "we are going to win" and "we are going to be the best in our business," and make sure everyone who joins the team becomes part of that plan.

All new employees are inducted into the culture that losing is not an option and that we will be number one in all we do. It becomes a way of life. That is why I liked to hire people who have played sports and loved competing. That type of person loves the battle, the fight, and the game. People who do not like confrontation do not do well in this type of environment. Somewhere in the history of every great company there was a visionary, an entrepreneur, a risk taker who charted the course to build that great company. Operating a great company once it is at the multibillion-dollar level does not take the same drive, the risk-taking skill, the guts—I could add a few other things but I think you get the point—as building the company from the beginning. Once that visionary, the man or woman with the plan, is no longer at the company things will change unless another entrepreneur replaces him or her. It may take a few different leaders before you have someone who really gets it and has what it takes to build an industry leader and a company that is known and branded as a great company. Without the right leader in place its growth will slow down and the services or product will deteriorate.

If you have the fire and passion and you have a good product or service, go make it happen! You can do it too!

eight

Meetings and Encounters with Leaders and Winners

There are special people we call super achievers who stand above others in business, politics, sports, and of course many other professions. These people have traits and characteristics that seem to push them to the top of whatever they do. There is no doubt that these super stars are worth studying and observing. You can learn from winners no matter what their profession. Many of them are entrepreneurs in their area of excellence, and they have built their own brands.

What I want to do in this chapter is share some of my personal encounters with a few of these super achievers. You may even be one of these people—you just have not had the chance to really find out. Sometimes it takes getting into the right place, position, or job before you find out that you too are one of the super achievers. It is kind of like giving a kid a paintbrush and finding out he has the skills of a real artist. Without putting the paintbrush in the child's hand you would never have known that he or she had that talent.

A great example that I experienced recently was with a student at a local high school. He was on the field during physical education class and the coach saw him pick up a football and easily throw it about seventy to eighty yards. When the coach asked him if he had ever played football he said no. He is now one of the quarterbacks on the team and throws the most beautiful passes I have ever seen a high school student throw. If the coach had not seen him throw the ball during a PE class he would not be playing football today.

There are people that you meet that you will never forget and the experience of meeting them will change your life. I want to share some experiences that I have had with those special individuals whose accomplishments are exceptional by anyone's standards. These people are different in ways that make them reach harder and further than others. Something about each one of them makes them very special in whatever area they are gifted. Some of these individuals excel in almost everything they choose to do.

Let me start with one of the most successful investors and money managers in the world who just happens to be one of the wealthiest men in the world. I had the very wonderful opportunity to have dinner with Warren Buffett not once but twice. I found him to be a very polite man who didn't mind sharing his thoughts on business, politics, or anything else you might want to talk about. He is very bright and extremely interesting to listen to. Both of the dinners were held at the late Senator Daniel Patrick Moynihan's condo in Washington, DC. At the table with me both times sat another CEO of a public company, a lobbyist, Senator Moynihan, and Warren Buffett. During both dinners I was given the opportunity and honor to sit next to Mr. Buffett. Senator Bob Kerrey of Nevada attended the second meeting and sat with us at the table. The discussions were all over the place as we sat there for two and a half hours after at least an hour of cocktails.

I remember this timing because I walked out of the condo with Warren and I looked at my watch and it was twelve midnight. I will never forget that day because it was also the day that *Forbes Magazine* had Warren on the front page as the richest man in America with a net worth of $25 billion and there I was hanging out with him talking politics and business. I had the chance to ask him about the different industries and companies that he invested in and why. I also got to talk to him about whom he liked in the next presidential race and why. We were able to discuss health care and health-care reform. I asked him about airplanes and his thoughts about companies buying them and flying their executives around the country. He explained that at one time he thought it was not such a good idea but that once he started using his own airplane he found a great savings in time and an increase in productivity. He talked about all the places he was able to travel to because of the plane. He fully understood when it was a waste of resources and when it was productive.

I also got to ask him about several of his favorite investments. We discussed his investment in Coca-Cola, and I asked him a question that, at the time, I thought was good but that afterward I realized I already knew the answer to.

He did not let me off easy for asking the dumb question. I asked him, "Why do you like Coke versus Pepsi?" The answer was simple: Coke is number one! What was I thinking? Boy, was that a dumb question. He also went into the two companies' strategies. He explained what he liked about Coke and what he thought about Pepsi's strategy. I sat there like a real nut thinking, "Did I really just ask Warren Buffett that question?"

We went on to have good conversation as he told me about the house he lived in and his car and airplane. He also let me know his support for the Democrats and gave me some thoughts on paying taxes. I found the entire conversation very interesting, and he certainly gave me some things to ponder. I still think about his comments to this day even though a decade has passed since the meeting. I heard on the news just the other day that his wealth is now over $70 billion. That is almost three times what it was the night I was with him and it was announced he was the richest man in America.

At the end of the night when we left the condo, Warren and I rode the elevator down to the street level together. When we walked outside a car was waiting for me. Warren just started walking down the dark street saying, "See you guys later." I looked at my friend Bob Elkins who was the CEO of another company and said, "Is he just going to walk down this street in the dark at midnight? Today he was on the front page of *Forbes* stating he is worth $25 billion and he is the richest man in America." So I yelled after Warren and said, "Wait up, Warren. I have a car, and I will give you a ride wherever you are going." He said,

"It's OK. I will catch a cab." I insisted that he let me give him a ride so he reluctantly got into the car and told the driver to take him to Georgetown.

Bob and I took him to a really nice gated home where he may have been staying and let him out. During the time that we'd driven through town, he was just one of the guys. We laughed and joked and took a couple of photos of us together and just enjoyed our time. He made us feel like we were his friends forever and that he enjoyed being with us that night. I certainly didn't think that less than a year later I would be invited to have dinner with him in Senator Moynihan's condo again.

Wow, what a great treat and another fun, entertaining evening. The senator was a great host, and it was really an honor to get to know him. He was very humble and supportive of all our conversations. Both times that I went to his home I remember seeing hanging on the hatrack his famous hat that he always wore when interviewed during the winter months in Washington, DC. I even thought about taking a photo of it just to show people that I had been to his home for dinner. (Only the older folks may even remember the senator and appreciate his famous hat.) His condo had a great view over the District, and as we looked out the large plate-glass window the senator would point out all the famous landmarks and places. He made sure the food, wine, and conversation never stopped flowing. He also was a super achiever, a former ambassador and sociologist, and many thought he was a super star in the way he handled many important meetings and relationships in

Washington. I found him to be a wonderful fellow with a tremendous amount of knowledge.

On my second dinner I spent a good bit of time talking with Senator Bob Kerrey, and I found him to be a humble, nice man who was very knowledgeable. He had many great ideas about what Washington should be doing to make this country great. I liked Bob Kerrey, and he was a good friend to me for many years. There was a fellow there whose first name was Eric who knew everyone. He was the catalyst that had brought us all together. I have to give Eric credit for those two great evenings. I don't know where he is today, but I would love to see him again.

While Warren and I were discussing his investments I asked him how he followed so many companies and billions of dollars in investments. He said what I expected him to say: "I have really good people under me that I trust to make good decisions." That was all I had to hear. All of you who will build a billion-dollar company will have to have good people under you whom you trust to make good decisions. This is a must, as you will have to learn to delegate if you are going to build something big. You cannot do it all. Not only can you not do it all but you cannot build anything very big unless you can delegate, and to do that you must have good, competent people or you will have things go wrong.

Another fellow that I found to be likeable but very different from Warren was Larry Ellison, CEO of Oracle. I had the opportunity to have a couple of meals and several meetings with Larry. Our first meeting was a lunch in one of his homes during which I got to hear his vision for Oracle, the new digital world, and how he saw other companies working with Oracle. I had another meeting in his offices where I got to meet his top people; this gave me real insight into the type of people he hired. I also got to interact with them, so I saw firsthand their aggressiveness and company spirit. I saw how talented they were and how they handled things in the negotiation process.

We had another meeting in my offices where we discussed the new digital health-care world and how our companies could partner together to build a state-of-the art digital hospital. We met again in a hotel suite in New York where we discussed the dollars and cents of our future relationship. Larry is very aggressive and is always working on the next deal and trying to move his company forward. He is very driven to be the best, and his success is the result of that drive and brain power. He also has some very good people working under him, and he has created a culture at Oracle that is infectious. That culture causes the company to continue its growth automatically to a certain extent because so many people are working to bring in business daily and grow the company. This automatic building of the company is a common and necessary trait among all great companies.

Larry and I had the opportunity to talk about the things we both like to do. I learned that we both are jet pilots and we have the same multi-engine instruments ratings, but we are also both single pilot rated in Citation jets. Being single pilot rated allows us to get into a jet and take off and fly it anywhere our hearts desire. Nothing much can compare with that freedom. Flying a jet airplane straight to 42,000 feet is quite exhilarating, as well as crossing this great country in the middle of the night watching the stars and the lights of great cities while traveling 480 miles an hour.

Extra activities like racing boats and flying airplanes keep the super achiever from getting bored and give the super achiever a reason to work so hard. You see, somehow in their minds they believe that if they work really hard then they have the right to play hard. There is also the challenge itself of flying the plane or catching the big fish, climbing the high mountain or racing the boat. Most chief executive officers, who are the entrepreneur type, love to have fun and prove that they are multi-talented. Why should people who do nothing but fly airplanes be the only ones who get to fly airplanes? They want to prove that they can do anything they put their mind to and that they are not limited to thinking about business or working in an office or doing some deal or merger.

Larry and I were interested in many of the same things, and we found a lot of common ground between us. We both believed in a more digital health-care world, which is now here. Almost everything he and I talked about has become a reality. We talked about building an electronic medical record before anyone else had ever built one. We talked about digital charting and billing. Well, today it is all digital and by law all medical records must be digital by 2014.

I guess it is also important to mention that I had the honor of meeting with four different US presidents and one of the most famous and loved presidents visited me at my home. That was Ronald Regan, and what a great gentleman he was to all of my family. I visited another president in the Oval Office and joined him on his private putting green and hit a few balls with him. We walked right out of the oval office and onto the putting green. What a great treat and a very special experience that I will never forget. I also had the great opportunity to spend time with two different speakers of our great House of Representatives and numerous congressman and senators as well as having a vice president visit with me at my home as well.

Vice President Dan Quayle and Richard Scrushy

I only share these experiences because they gave me a chance to see our country's leadership up close and to understand what made these leaders different from others in leadership positions and politics. Politicians and chief executive officers have a lot in common, yet they are very different. Politicians are outgoing and usually outspoken people, but they are not risk takers and instead tend to work themselves into relationships and special favors to get the things they want to get done while in office. A really strong CEO just couldn't stomach the process of all the positioning to accomplish what little they get done.

Chief executive officers make things happen daily, and they see results relatively quickly in the financial performance of their companies. You would never see a CEO allow his company to spend more than it takes in unless they were in a building or start-up phase. For example, please tell me how our leadership in Congress approves a situation that takes in $2 trillion and spends $3 trillion? Leadership in the political area is very different from building a company where you have to hire good people, make sales, and manage profits while branding and marketing a company's products. I have met so many chief executive officers who are very up-front about the fact that they could never serve in a political office. This is a real problem because what we need in Washington are men and women who fully understand how to make a profit and control expenses and to budget your expenses and stay within that budget.

I was the CEO of a Fortune 500 company. As such, I associated with and attended conferences with other Fortune 500 chief executive officers, and, believe me, that was a crowd you definitely would want to hang out with. I consider that a major highlight of my life and career.

Imagine sitting at the table having lunch with the chairman and CEO of the largest hotel chain in the world or the largest pharmaceutical company or one of the largest retailers in the world. Not to mention the largest banks and financial institutions. I remember the cocktail parties and standing in the room with hundreds of chief executive officers from the top five hundred companies in America. The conversations ranged from politics, markets, boats, airplanes, and world travel to golf and sports. There was incredible energy in the room and extreme drive and brain power everywhere. These men and women were serious about success and making big strides. They were all very focused on what they wanted to achieve, and they had their opinions on what was good about this world and what was wrong with it.

I want to impress upon you that there is something very special about people who have the leadership skills and talent to build great companies, a unique trait that anyone who has a chance to interact with one of these people will recognize. You will know if you are one of these people as you begin to build your company. Sometimes I even wonder if it is a curse, as you are always about your business trying to build something. It is as if you do not know how to really relax. For example, I never take a nap. I do not ever stop and just sit still. I constantly look for the next business deal, the next new company, concept, or idea. I also think that when you have this unique trait that you are also always on the lookout for talent—people who can help you build companies because those people are hard to find. Few exist and there are fewer still that will stand with you from the beginning to the end. You cannot do it by yourself.

Only certain individuals are perfectly geared to be the number two or three in a company; not everyone can be the quarterback and call the plays, but you cannot win without a good team. All your key positions are important. Once you understand the process of building a great business, then you will know when you meet the real entrepreneur who can get the job done. When you hear the business plan presentation and you listen to the passion of the visionary you will know that this one can do it. Sometimes the concept and the idea may not be the greatest but the right entrepreneur can turn it into a good business—for example, the product that was out of patent that I discussed in an earlier chapter.

Having met so many people in leadership positions, both in politics and business, I believe that I understand and can recognize the real deal when I meet with the person and hear what he or she has to say. Even though the person has the vision, the drive, and the talent, in most cases that person will still need coaching and counseling on other things in order to build the great billion-dollar company. The person may still need help in putting in the systems, hiring the right people, and handling all the financial and legal issues. I found that many times I just needed someone to bounce things off of; someone older with a little more wisdom and gray hair was always valuable.

Another category of leaders and real competitors are professional athletes. These guys have the great energy to fight and fight and fight. You can learn from the determination of a great athlete to win. I remember Heisman Trophy winner Bo Jackson telling me that every time he went into the huddle he would tell the quarterback to give the ball to him. He wanted to run; he believed he could score the points necessary to win because he believed in himself. When he was playing baseball he said every time the batter got up to bat he hoped the batter would hit the ball to him.

I remember times when we had many hard phone calls that needed to be made and I would tell my people to give me the numbers and I would call them first thing in the morning and get it done. This is an attitude that a successful CEO must have. Make the tough calls and make them early. I always felt so relieved after making the tough calls, and they were never as bad as I thought they would be and the results were typically positive.

Even though I have never been a great golfer I have played golf with a lot of great golfers and super achievers. I played four or five rounds with Michael Jordan and several with Charles Barkley. I have played with many of the great pros such as Jack Nicklaus and Chi Chi Rodriguez. One of my best golfing buddies was Randy Owen of the country group Alabama. One of the most memorable golf games I ever played was with Jane Seymour, the actress, as my partner. Wow, what a wonderful lady and a good golfer—she beat me and she played off the men's tees. I played with Tom Glavine, pitcher for the Atlanta Braves, once in a tournament. What concentration he had! No small talk with him, as he was out to win. Having spent time with many great athletes has given me another look at being competitive. I have spent time with the likes of Emmitt Smith, Dan Marino, Troy Aikman, Kyle Petty, Cory Everson, Doug Heir, Matt Barr, Brett Favre, Johnny Unitas, Bart Starr, Lex Luger, Herschel Walker, Muhammad Ali, Michael Jordan, Bo Jackson, Charles Barkley, and more than fifty other great athletes over the years. I witnessed the great drive that all of these men and women possessed that set them apart as winners.

There is so much that we as chief executive officers can learn about getting up after a fall from these aggressive competitors. If you can take the hit and the fall and get up and keep going back and you never give up, you can build that great company just like you have the chance to become a great athlete. Of course, like an athlete, we know you must have the ability and the skills to start with. We will get injured on occasion, but we can learn how to come back from the injury, just like the athlete. And the aggressiveness of an athlete can carry you through your competitive battles.

I have also had the opportunity because of my love of music to get to know a lot of great musicians, many who became stars. One of my most memorable times with a great musician and singer was the day my wife and I spent with Garth Brooks. We picked up him, his wife, and his manager at the airport in Atlanta and flew to Washington, DC, on our plane together. We were with our dear beloved friend, the late great Donna Hilley, who was president of Sony Tree Publishing. I went to a dinner with Garth where he gave an ASCAP award to Billy Joel.

Man, talk about a great night. I found myself in a meeting over dinner with Billy Joel and Garth Brooks. Now, tell me, how in the world do you think that was? I found them both to be really nice guys, smart but also very aggressive.

Garth is a very good businessman who has his act together. He and I talked about the liability of running his business. He told me about the workers comp issues he'd had with his team rigging his concerts. I was impressed with his knowledge and understanding of business. We had a good bit of time on the plane to talk business. My wife and I were blessed with lots of fun experiences like this one. Again, here was one of the most famous entertainers in the world, and I had the chance to get into his space and see what made him tick—what an opportunity to learn. This man had a good plan, and he was working it. No doubt he is truly an entrepreneurial country music singer.

We could talk about others like Reba McEntire and the group Alabama with their forty-two number one hits. There are so many talented people in the music business who are smart and aggressive enough to take their talent and turn it into a great business that makes them millions of dollars. What is real about these performers and singers is that they must have the talent to sing and perform as well as understand the business side or have a manager or someone who will help and direct them. I was fortunate to meet and get to know many artists over the years as well as one of the best-known attorneys in the music business, Joel Katz, who has been a dear friend for years. Joel introduced me to Tommy Matolla, former president of Sony Music, and Emilio Estefan, music producer and husband of Gloria Estefan. I had a wonderful opportunity to get to know these guys as we all served together on the board of Gibson Guitars.

We will always find out that, at the end of the day, the drive and the vision must be there. If you are to be successful in anything and if you are going down the road to build a billion-dollar company, you really have to have the spirit that you are going to do this no matter what, and there is nothing else that you want to do more. That is a winning spirit, and it will take you through the hard times that you will most definitely experience as you build your company.

The scripture says all good gifts come from God, and I am a firm believer that we are all given gifts. But if we choose not to use those gifts we may lose them. For example, if you are given the talent to sing or play a sport and you choose not to use that gift and develop it, you will lose it. Even someone as talented as Tiger Woods has to practice golf and stay in shape to be able to operate in that gift. If you have the talent to be a builder of businesses then you need to be operating in that gift. If you are in a job today and you are unhappy with the way the company is being managed and the way the leadership operates, you may be in the wrong place. The message here is that if you can see the right way to do things, then maybe you should be building a company yourself. This is exactly how I found out that I was an entrepreneur and a builder of businesses.

As I grew up through the ranks of an NYSE company and was promoted numerous times for my accomplishments I began to realize that I could do these things myself and that I didn't need to be working for someone else. There was a day when I walked into my boss's office with $5 million in contracts for him to sign, and he said, "Why should I sign these when you know more about this than I do?" That day he told me that he was raising my approval limit to $5 million. I signed the contracts and walked out realizing that I could run the whole company and that it was time for me to leave and start my own. I guess that gave me the confidence to do what I was called to do and to use the gift that had been given to me to build companies. I never turned back after that day, and I had no fear as I knew what I had to go do and I knew nothing would stop me from building my own company.

I meet people all the time who are not operating in their gift, and I know that there are a lot of frustrated people working in jobs where they are very unhappy. Many times it is because they have the talent to do bigger and better things. You do not have to be the sole entrepreneur on your own to be happy or to operate in your gift, but you do need to be working in a company that allows you to use whatever your gift is. You may have a great mind for marketing or being a salesman, a graphic artist, a writer, or a brilliant finance person. You want to make sure that whatever your talent or gift is that you are using it in a productive way. So many people live miserable lives because they never operate in their gift, so they never truly find their destiny and purpose in life.

As I look back at all the people who were placed into my life at different times I realize now how strategic many of them were. For example, so many of them taught me valuable things that I needed to know in order to be able to do the things I had to do to build the billion-dollar company. I can start with my parents teaching me to be strong and encouraging me to always work hard and be the best I could be at whatever I did. Then I had an instructor in college whose words were a turning point for me. He told me that I had the potential to do great things but that I had to get into a productive mode in my life—I had to stop fighting with people and start working with them. Wow, was that important. That one little conference was so special to me. It totally changed who I was, and it seemed that I grew up into a new man at that moment and found a new level of maturity. I was changed, and it was all for the good.

We have to pay attention to the connections we make in life and the people who are put into our path. Many of them are door openers for us, and we have to be able to recognize them when they come. A couple of the senior managers and officers of the first NYSE company that I worked for taught me a great deal that I had to know in order to begin to build a billion-dollar company. I believe this book has a purpose and that it can help many who are still struggling to determine if they have the gift to build their own company.

I know now that many of the people who came to work for me have gone on to build successful companies themselves. Things happen for a reason, and I believe there is no doubt that some of those people learned from me and the team that we assembled to build our billion-dollar company.

Just be aware of your encounters and look for the purpose in them. The other point in this chapter is that we can learn from great athletes and leaders and successful people as we observe and study their drive and commitment. Without the kind of dedication that these winners have you will not make it to your goal of building a billion-dollar company.

Left to right, Warren Buffett, Senator Bob Kerrey, Senator Daniel Patrick Moynihan, and Richard Scrushy

nine

Making the Difference

I have given a great deal of thought to what it really takes to build a successful billion-dollar company, and I will attempt to articulate that in this chapter. I will try to avoid repeating things that I've discussed in the previous chapter about encounters with leaders and winners but there will be a little crossover that cannot be helped.

We have covered several different topics in this book, but I want you to know that the attitude, work ethic, leadership, drive, personal management techniques, and your personal limits regarding spending, buying, selling, merging, acquiring, consolidating, and building are going to determine whether or not you will make it to the billion-dollar level. Most people just can't work at the level of intensity that it takes to build an idea or vision into a large successful billion-dollar business. The focus on making it happen may cause others to talk about your aggressive management style because they do not understand what you are doing or what it is that you will have to do in order to achieve your goal.

In one company I had meetings every Monday with the management, and many of them still talk about the meetings to this day. This was the time the members of the management team got their instructions and were held accountable for doing their job. You must get your people to do the jobs you hired them to do. This means you must hold them accountable and have some way of checking their work and productivity as well as some way of communicating to them what it is that they need to be doing.

I found that since some of them may not understand the plan, you may have to set their priorities for them or they will do as they think best. Some will take the easy road rather than doing the hard stuff that will really take your company to the highest level. You must understand that a lot of people are content with a job, and when they leave work at five they turn off their brain when it comes to your company. Most of them do not understand where you are going or the long-term game plan.

Some will criticize you for having a meeting where you explain to them what you need them to be doing. I often wondered why they didn't just leave and go somewhere else. But the bottom line is that they are not sure what they should be doing, and sometimes their response is to complain and buck the leadership. As I reflect back on some of the personalities I worked with in the past who were troublemakers and complainers I get a little upset at myself for letting them stay around as long as I did. I can see now how disruptive they were, and in most cases they spent a lot of their time creating problems rather than solutions.

I have talked a lot about management issues to include systems and controls and how to hire winners. All of this is so important, but if you cannot get your people to do the things that you need them to do then you will not achieve your goal of building the billion-dollar company. How do you do this? You have to stay on top of everything that will get you to the level you are targeting. You have to have someone working for you who can help you stay on top of the reports, and that person must help to organize your life so you do not miss things.

You must create an environment that makes your people competitive with each other in terms of work product and productivity. They need to be trying to outperform each other all the time. When you go into meetings the winners should shine and the losers should stand out so that they either get up to the level of the winners or they get moved out. Performance is most important and winning is everything. Some of the people who worked for me hated being held accountable and having to be competitive in order to become a winner. So many people just want to cruise through life doing what they want to do rather than what you need them to do. You cannot let them decide the pace at which they will work and what they want to work on. You have to have a major handle on what your employees are doing as a whole. Think about a group of ants building an ant bed. Have you ever watched them? They work together as a team and they all move at the speed necessary to keep things moving at the pace that they need to move to stay in line and not run each other over. You want to create a company where there is a good team effort to move the company forward without having a key person falling down on the job. If you can get everyone working at a good pace doing the job that they need to be doing then you will be able to build a great company.

Watching the ants is interesting because you never see an ant getting out of line and doing its own thing. The ants know the plan and they all follow it. You will have some try to do their own thing and they will even try to get others to go with them. You will have to deal with those employees if they continue to be disruptive and destructive to your plan. Many times they do not understand that you have the vision and you are the risk taker. You are the visionary and the one who sees the future and knows the plan.

As I reflect on what it really takes to build industry leaders that become multibillion-dollar companies I think about the super-charged personalities and drive required to build those companies. It is as if they have a turbo charger hooked to their brain. I know that I never stopped thinking of building it bigger and better and more profitable, but that is what is required in order to build the billion-dollar company. Some people get nervous around these personalities because they feel they are reading your mind as you talk to them. They already know what you are going to say and they know exactly how to get what they want from you. If you do not have anything to add to their plans then it was nice seeing you and go have a great life.

I have work to do and there is no such thing as enough. You can't ever make enough money because the money is no longer what makes them tick. It is truly the control of the business and the grand slams that make them get up every day. It fuels them to be creative and apply large amounts of pressure on lots of people daily. How are you really going to build a billion in revenues if you are not thinking every minute of the day and putting a lot of pressure on all of your employees and pushing them to give all they have all the time?

The founder, visionary, and CEO carries a heavy load daily and no one can understand it unless they have personally been there and experienced it themselves. The pressure builds over time and you never get it off of you. It is something you carry twenty-four hours a day every day. No matter if you are at the beach or on a boat or playing golf the pressure is always with you. I found it affected my golf game because I couldn't let go. I was always focused on building the company, the work and deals that needed to be completed, and I never wanted to stop thinking about it. It was a large part of me and I was driven by the opportunities and the challenges.

The pressure can affect who you are and who you become over time. It affects your relationship with your family and your friends. People will see the personality changes and some will even tell you about it. But this will not change who you are because the company and its success is far more important than what they are telling you. You have a big payroll and you worry about the people and their families; however, most people do not understand that. You begin to carry that load. You worry about the children as you meet them and the spouses and you think if you fail they will be hurt. They all depend on you making it happen, and that is a pressure that many may not understand.

Organizing your life will be very important if you are going to achieve the goal of building a billion-dollar company. I found organizing your time will help increase your productivity by volumes. For example, a good time to work out, which is essential to your productivity, is before everyone else gets up. I found that starting my morning workout at 4:45 a.m. worked really well for me: a one-hour workout of thirty minutes of weights and stretching and thirty minutes of cardio. This allowed for a shower and a protein breakfast and by seven o'clock I was on my way to work. But don't neglect morning time with the family, which is also essential on a regular basis. I always tried to be at the office when others arrived. I found that to be very important in order to keep the work pace and productivity at a high level. Working out and staying fit will increase your ability to work, think, and to process large volumes of work product—plus I found that it keeps you upbeat all day. On days that I didn't at least do the cardio I felt sluggish and could not push myself at the same level as I could on the days I exercised.

I also tried to eat lunch in the office, and when I had guests I would have lunch brought in. When we eventually exceeded the billion-dollar level at one company we added an executive dining room where all the senior guys could eat lunch together. That was a great idea as we were able to do business during that time that otherwise would have been downtime. Using every minute that you have during the day to move all the projects along and push people by asking questions about their work, creating expectations that these objectives have deadlines, keeps the momentum going and everyone working hard to meet the plans and deadlines.

One of the biggest challenges I found with keeping things moving forward was wasting time in nonproductive meetings. Others may want to meet with you about some need they have that has nothing to do with building your business. Often your own people want to use the meeting to give you reasons why they can't do the hard things that have to be done in order to achieve your goals. My experience is that when things come up that you really hate to do or you dread doing because of the possibility of failing or being turned down you have to do those things first. I would go into work and immediately start making the toughest calls and have the meetings that I dreaded. I wanted to get those things out of the way so I could focus on everything else.

You can't let things get you down. You will find that you worry too much, and usually things are not as bad as you think they will be. Many times when I had one of my key people tell me some horrible reason why we could not do something or if they told me about how hard it was going to be to get something done I would get on the phone and just move it forward or make the tough calls myself. I was usually able to get the difficult things done. It will teach your people that you have got to push and believe in what you can do and to go ahead and do the difficult things and make the tough calls. Sometimes you just have to be super strong and stand for what you know is right and what has to be done in order to achieve your goals.

Be very careful about how you address your people. I have seen some really horrible chief executive officers who depress their people and make them hate working for them. Leadership is so essential to success. If you cannot motivate your people and create a powerful team that will help move the company and the big deals up the mountain you will not be able to achieve your goals. This comes naturally to most great leaders, and this may make the difference between a great visionary and a great leader who really can build the billion-dollar company. You have heard that success is dependent on management, management, management, and I am telling you that it also takes leadership, leadership, leadership!

In order to lead you must be able to follow and you must know when to lead and when to follow. When you have one of your employees' give you a good idea make sure you encourage them by recognizing that person in management meetings. Use their ideas to improve your business. When they see you follow them or their idea, you will see a committed and dedicated employee with a positive attitude. You also know that positive attitudes in companies increase productivity and they are infectious. Let your people know that you appreciate their ideas and help. You have to motivate them to be productive thinkers like you. If you think you can do it all you will fail. Ask the guy that works on the loading dock the best way to run the loading dock and you may learn a few things. When you conduct your management meetings talk about the good things first that are going right and let your hard workers know that you appreciate all they do. Adults worry about their jobs because many have families to feed and support and they want to do the right things so they can keep their jobs and not have to worry. It really reduces stress on them when they know that they are doing what you want them to do. Once you have everyone on the team properly motivated tell them what the challenges are and what is going wrong and give them solutions as you see them. But never leave the meeting without getting their suggestions and ideas. This is where you may learn something again. Also remember to always leave the meeting on an upbeat positive thought. Speak victory and success into your business and management team.

ten

When Blessed, Bless Others

Make Sure There Is Balance in Your Life

There is no way that I could write a book about building a successful business without discussing the concept of charitable giving or philanthropy. Most successful people are generous, and they understand the concept of helping others. When blessed we must bless others less fortunate than we are. Follow the big gifts and on the other end of the gift you will find someone who has had a considerable amount of financial success in his or her life. The only other person you might find at the end of that gift is someone born into a wealthy family or a descendant of a very financially successful person.

One of the most important things we can do in our lives is to help others less fortunate. As a leader in the corporate community, charitable giving and philanthropy will become part of your success and it will be expected by other corporate leaders. When your big company starts making large profits you will want to make sure you become a supporter of community projects and charitable organizations. So many wealthy and successful people forget what is most important in life. Making this world a better place to live by helping others should be one of your priorities.

What is this life really all about? Why are we here? Can we take our winnings with us when we die? No, we cannot. I remember going to my father's house after he passed away, cleaning out his closet and gathering up all of his things. When I first got to his house I looked around. There was his car and truck and tractor, and then when I went into his house I saw all his favorite things. All of it was there for whomever wanted to take them. Some of the things he left to certain children, but most of the things he owned were just sitting there. None of his stuff went with him, and at that moment I seriously realized that all my stuff would be doing the same thing when I passed on. Most of us know that, but it really hits home when someone close to you dies.

So what is all this stuff about? Why do we spend all our lives in pursuit of so many things? It seems senseless when you really think about it. I remember people saying whoever ends up with the most toys wins, but now I think whoever ends up with your toys wins because you paid for them and they get them free. At my still-young age of sixty-one I am not too interested in having many things or much stuff. It is just not as important as I thought it was when I was younger. The less stuff we have the more time we have in our lives. I am beginning to think you have to be a certain age to truly understand this. You would never have convinced me of that when I was in my thirties and forties.

When I went through my father's things I began to realize that he had been getting rid of things for some time, and it hit me that he really understood this as well. He only had five suits, about ten shirts, and two or three pairs of dress shoes. I only spent about thirty minutes gathering up his things. My father was a successful man who could have bought anything he wanted. He did drive a Mercedes and he always had a new truck and a nice tractor that he used on his farm. He began to realize as he got older that owning a bunch of things and collecting stuff was not so important anymore. So I think he truly realized that less really is more. But I also noticed something else. He began to give more and more to projects in his community. I recall once when a tornado came through his little town and ripped several homes apart. He searched out the people who lived in the houses that were damaged. If they didn't have insurance he gave them the money they needed to rebuild their homes. He gifted more to his church and he donated to other charities. He began to realize that he couldn't take it with him and he wanted to help others.

One of the best lessons my father ever taught me was the importance of tithing or giving to the church. When I was just a little fellow, maybe only five or six years old, my dad would give me the check or envelope with the money in it each week to put into the offering plate at church. I remember asking him once why he gave money to the church when our family needed money for things. I will never forget him telling me that first you have to give back to God for the many blessings that He continued to give to our family, and I would have to say we were blessed in many ways. We had a roof over our heads and a wonderful mother who loved us all dearly. My parents spent a lot of time teaching us the things necessary to build a strong understanding of how we should live our lives and they grounded us with a foundation necessary to help get us through the ups and downs and trials of life.

I guess my point of all of this is that we can't let the stuff control us—we have to control it. I believe that if I had it to do over, I would have given more and bought less. It is very true that having enough money to buy the finer things in life is great, but put it all in perspective and make sure you have some reason and balance in your life. I will also say that this comes from experience, as I was guilty of acquiring too much stuff. Too many toys will cause you to spend too much time away from what may be most important in your life. I found myself focused on taking care of all the things that I owned and not spending that time with my family. It also took me away from focusing on the business to some degree. When you buy the toys you will want to spend time playing with them, and, believe me, the cost and maintenance will always be much more than you thought or planned.

So add some balance in your life, and do some good to help others. Find some charities that you can grow with and become close to. There are so many needs and so much suffering in this world. You will not have to look far to find people who need your financial blessings. That return will be more important to you as you grow older. Do not forget your local church. According to scripture we should all put God first in our lives, and that means giving back to Him some of what He has given to us. Just read Malachi 3:8–12 and you will get the picture of what we are called to do and what we are promised.

Corporate giving and philanthropy is expected in most corporate circles. It is a great way to brand your company within your community and to get to know the movers and shakers in your city and state or even larger movers and shakers on a national scale once your company is large enough to make the really big national donations. Also remember there are tax benefits to corporate giving.

Being part of the charitable giving community can open doors that otherwise can't be opened. I found myself on boards sitting next to people I did not think I would have ever had a chance to meet, much less talk to. Several deals came from the time I spent at charitable functions. I also was able to learn about others and how they achieved their success. My wife and I had a chance to meet their spouses and in many cases we became friends. There was no doubt a big return for our support of charitable organizations and our giving.

I am a firm believer that blessings come from blessings, and I know that even though I have had some tough spots in my life I am a blessed man. I believe that these blessings come from the blessings my family has given to others. It is a good idea to have a plan once you are in a position financially to begin your philanthropy. Different needs will come up and you will have to support those needs, but an organized approach is necessary to giving and I highly recommend that you put some serious thought into that plan.

The giving and philanthropy is all part of the success of your company, and it will be expected within the corporate community. It can do a lot of good for both you and your company.

Plant some great seeds, and watch them grow as you water them over the years. It is all part of building your billion-dollar company.

I hope you are blessed in your business venture and that one day you find yourself at the top of a billion-dollar company!

If you have further questions or would like assistance in helping you build your billion-dollar company you can go to my website **richardscrushy.com** or **7venthpower. com.** Send us your contact information and some details about your company and we will contact you.

If you are interested in having me speak or give a presentation you can contact me at the same websites. Go to these websites to learn more about 7venth Power, Inc.

About the Author

Richard Scrushy was born in 1952 in a small Southern town. He grew up in Selma, Alabama, and at a young age, as he attended high school, he worked at various jobs, played baseball, and performed in a local rock and roll band. Mr. Scrushy is a graduate of Jefferson State Community College and the University of Alabama in Birmingham and holds honorary doctorates from University of Alabama, Troy University, and Birmingham Southern College. He is well known as a dynamic and successful entrepreneur for founding, building, and serving as chairman and CEO of two Fortune 500 companies, both listed on the NYSE and both having revenues in the billions of dollars. He also founded, financed, and served as chairman of another NYSE company that he merged with another company once it reached the billion-dollar mark. Mr. Scrushy was involved in assisting in the founding and funding of many other companies over a twenty-year period. During that time as chairman and CEO of one of his companies he completed approximately $7 billion in acquisitions of which many were other public companies. That company became one of the largest health-care companies geographically in America—with more than 2,350 locations operating in every major city in the country, all fifty states, the United Kingdom, Saudi Arabia, Puerto Rico, and Australia. The company employed more than fifty-two thousand people and was branded as a quality cost-effective health-care company. Also during that time he was involved in hundreds of acquisitions with the three companies for which he served as chairman. He also was involved in raising billions of dollars in debt and equity for those companies.

Mr. Scrushy has served on numerous boards, including HealthSouth Corporation, Caremark, Capstone Capital, Integrated Health Services, Russ Pharmaceuticals, Gibson Guitars, Alabama Sports Hall of Fame, University of Alabama, Troy University, and Birmingham Southern College.

Mr. Scrushy is a business advisor, commercial multiengine instrument pilot, musician, songwriter, motivational and inspirational speaker, author, and minister. He enjoys spending time with his wife, Leslie, his nine children, and his seven grandchildren.

For more information or to contact Mr. Scrushy visit www.7Venthpower.com or www.richardscrushy.com.